THIRTEEN PERSISTENT
ECONOMIC FALLACIES

THIRTEEN PERSISTENT ECONOMIC FALLACIES

E. J. Mishan

Westport, Connecticut
London

Library of Congress Cataloging-in-Publication Data

Mishan, E. J. (Edward J.), 1917–
   Thirteen persistent economic fallacies / E.J. Mishan.
     p. cm.
   Sequel to the author's 21 popular economic fallacies.
   Includes bibliographical references and index.
   ISBN 978–0–313–36605–5 (alk. paper)
   1. Economics. I. Mishan, E. J. (Edward J.), 1917– 21 popular economic fallacies. II. Title.
HB171.M545 2009
330—dc22   2008045459

British Library Cataloguing in Publication Data is available.

Library of Congress Catalog Card Number: 2008045459
ISBN: 978–0–313–36605–5

First published in 2009

Praeger Publishers, 88 Post Road West, Westport, CT 06881
An imprint of Greenwood Publishing Group, Inc.
www.praeger.com

Printed in the United States of America

The paper used in this book complies with the
Permanent Paper Standard issued by the National
Information Standards Organization (Z39.48–1984).

10 9 8 7 6 5 4 3 2 1

To Etty Harris

(a.k.a. the Mother Teresa of Golders Green)

CONTENTS

PREFACE

This volume is a sequel to my *Twenty-One Popular Economic Fallacies,* which appeared in 1970. The reduction in the number of economic fallacies in this present volume is to be explained partly by the fact that quite a few economic issues that loomed large during the 1960s—including American economic domination, the payroll tax (erroneously believed to encourage investment), the so-called brain-drain, and a number of fallacies about the ameliorative powers of economic growth—seem to have slipped below the horizon of public concern. The other part of the explanation, however, is my decision to treat the more persistent current fallacies in greater depth.

One of the consequences of rapid economic growth in the West over the past half century is a rising level of anxiety and stress, unavoidably perhaps in view of the increasing pace and complexity of modern life—shaped as it is by the ruthless advance of technological innovation—which appears to be moving counter to the intuitive needs of ordinary mortals.

Another consequence of postwar economic growth is the more visible impact of the state on our lives and the haste of modern governments to enact legislation, often enough in response to social problems that emerge from the popular diffusion of technological innovations. This spiraling need to cram ever more legislation into a session of Congress leaves governments with less time and patience to fully consider and explain to the public the range of consequences that are expected to follow from the measures they hope to adopt, except in a rather superficial way that is aimed to encourage consensus or at least acquiescence. Too often, this takes the form of assuring the public that the government has taken expert advice or that it has consulted at length with all groups that would be directly affected by the proposed legislation. And to crown it all, we can depend upon it that the senator or representative concerned with the legislation will assure us that it is in "the national interest."

Now if the policies that governments today seek to implement had only limited impact on our well-being, their impatience to "get on with the job" would not matter that much. But, as suggested above, much of recent legislation that produces restrictions and regulations on our lives does indeed affect our well-being. What is more, the nature of events, regional and global, may be assuming a critical magnitude. It is no longer a gross exaggeration to assert that we are close to the brink of ecological disaster, a consequence chiefly of the eruption of world population over the past century accompanied as it is by the spread of new disruptive technologies. The mounting spillover effects generated by the adoption of new technologies by industry range from growing congestion of motorized traffic in our cities and highways to the current ethical and religious conflicts that can be traced to the recent availability of "liberating" innovations of medical science: from the threat of nuclear annihilation to a more gradual demise of human life on the planet should the protective ozone layer continue to dissipate. In these circumstances, political decisions taken by governments the world over may have the most dire and distressing consequences on human societies.

Be this as it may, the lack of informed discussion these days on important economic issues is largely the result of members of both government and opposition being prone to the influences still exerted by obsolescent "forward-looking" liberal doctrines. It is certainly disconcerting to discover that in these turbulent times the country continues to be governed by people whose political responses are guided by economic presumptions that can no longer be vindicated; people who regard as self-evident that any increase in the rate of economic growth (as conventionally measured), any increase in peoples' mobility, any increase of the country's exports, or expansion in the number of university students, and so on, must bring us the sooner into the millennium. Yet it is just because such economic propositions are accepted without question by the establishment, indeed by much of the educated public, that current debates on economic issues tend to be ill-informed or superficial.

To be sure, the lack of informed debate among the literate public can also be blamed on the professional economist, not only for neglecting to provide it with a clear understanding of the implications of economic policies being proposed or pursued, but also for neglecting to apprise it of alternative policies that are better able to realize the apparently desired ends. For unaided in this respect, the public cannot be expected to penetrate the smoke screen of economic mysticism spun by "experts" in order to justify the predilections of the government that employs them.

Certainly, the Executive branch of the U.S. government is not unknown to employ or consult economists believed to be sympathetic to its doctrinal views. Even if the economist who agrees to advise the government does not himself have any initial preconceptions about politically acceptable economic proposals, he may find himself gradually edging towards those that do. The prompting of ambition, a quite natural desire to feel he is of some use to the ministers he serves, the need to get along with associates, with civil servants and politicians, all incline him to start thinking about economic issues in terms of what is politically feasible. For example, he may well believe that a variable or "floating" exchange rate for currency (perhaps along with certain safeguards) offers a better solution to the balance-of-payments problem than measures taken to maintain a fixed rate of exchange. Yet if he learns from experience, or from the assurances of associates, that a variable exchange rate is "just not on," he knows that he can only annoy political decision makers to no purpose by insisting on bringing his private views on the subject into official discussions. Rather than take the risk of being resented or ignored, he will come to terms with the existing political constraints on the range of practical economic alternatives. Abiding by such constraints he will in time come to be regarded by the government, indeed by the establishment, as a "sound" man, a moderate and practical economist, one who can be relied upon to tender sensible economic advice.

Given such political realities, there is indeed a need for the concerned public to become better informed on economic matters.

One way of achieving this desideratum is to adopt the practice, once current in the United States, where top-flight economists would turn from their fascination with arcane academic issues being fathomed in the professional journals for the express purpose of clarifying topical economic issues, so enabling the intelligent citizen better to appraise alternative solutions and so to contribute to a more informed debate.

Thus, without bandying jargon or resorting to formulas, the economist—indeed the scientist generally, whether of physics or chemistry—without being either condescending or superficial, should be able to communicate to the public the nature of the consequences that can be expected to flow, under given conditions, from a given action or program. Moreover, in the case of the economist at least, he can also reveal in an informal way the chain of logic by which he reaches his conclusions.

A complementary procedure, that pursued here, is to expose the concerned citizen to the shock-treatment of discovering that much of what passes for conventional economic wisdom is in fact fallacious. If the former approach has the advantage of dealing with topical issues, the latter (adopted here) has the advantage of greater depth of treatment and may therefore have more appeal to the intelligent citizen who does not have the time or the inclination to pore over economic textbooks. But, as already indicated, the two approaches are obviously complementary. Both have much to contribute to the growth among the populace of habitual and articulate criticism that is the bane of governments and the lifeblood of democracy.

It would be presumptuous to believe that a volume devoted to exposing the more persisting economic fallacies, even if received with favor by the public, would go far from exorcising them from society. As Sir Thomas Browne observes in his *Religio Medici:*

> Heresies perish not with their Authors but, like the river Arethusa though they lose their currents in one place, they rise up in another. One General Council is not able

to extirpate one single Heresie; it may cancell'd for the present; but revolution of time, and the like aspects from Heaven, will restore it, when it will flourish till it be condemned again.

I am therefore resigned to discover that mere exposure of an economic fallacy will not be enough to expunge it from acceptance by society, and that it will continue to find comfortable lodging in the conventional wisdom. Yet I might reasonably hope that this volume will serve to ruffle complacency among politicians and officials, and that a number of postwar orthodoxies—such as the increase in society's welfare from sustained economic growth, the economic benefits to the nation of immigrant labor, or the burden we have to shoulder from increasing the national debt—be clearly exposed for the humbug they are.

In talking of fallacies I use the word in its broader sense to cover unsound or erroneous arguments as well as false notions about the economic universe, and I extend it occasionally to encompass an incomplete appreciation of the complexity of the problem (as in the chapter on the economic consequences of forming a common market).

Having laid out my remit, I may now claim, with perhaps only a modicum of perverse pride, that nearly all of my chosen fallacies move in the most respectable circles. They have appeared in the speeches of members of both Houses of Congress, in the solemn utterances of cabinet secretaries, and in the leader columns of *The New York Times, The Economist,* and other respectable newspapers and journals. More commonly, however, the fallacy in question takes the surreptitious form of being the implied premise underlying some proposed policy measure. I have, nonetheless, forborne from "naming names," as it would be quite unfair to do so. The fallacies I treat here are, with one exception, neither "stupid" nor careless; in fact, they are quite plausible, and the intelligent citizen can be forgiven for subscribing to them. But they are, alas, influential in shaping public opinion on important issues.

Some explanatory remarks may be useful in assuring those readers who are strong for "realism" that the simple constructs in the chapters that follow will indeed suffice in drawing valid conclusions. I am fully aware of this seemingly "Ivory Tower" method employed by theoretical economists in broaching economic problems—the "let-us-suppose this" and then "let-us-suppose that" way of conducting an economic analysis. The reader may well jib at conclusions drawn from what looks like excessive simplification that may thought to evade the complexities of the real world.

Now if the economist were engaged in *describing* how people actually behave in the real world, such misgiving may be justified. But in fact the economist maintains that the only *relevant* premises, even though they be simplified assumptions, are those premises from which the conclusions or generalizations derived are themselves vindicated by the empirical evidence. Hence, so long as all the generalizations that can logically be derived from the adopted premises are not contradicted by the empirical evidence, such adopted premises will continue to be used. All economic generalizations, however, are restricted by what is called the *ceteris paribus* clause; that is, by the requirement that "other things be equal" or, rather, that other (closely related) things remain unchanged.

It transpires, however, that apart from one fundamental axiom, there is only one behavioral assumption that has to be tacitly accepted in the following chapters. As for the axiom mentioned, it is inherent in the conceptual foundation of mainstream economics, one that can be traced back to the revolution in theoretical economics that occurred in 1870, which effectively dethroned Adam Smith's labor theory of value by a subjective theory of value. Thenceforth the value of a good to a person was to be measured by the largest sum he is willing to pay for it: the value of a "bad" by the minimal sum the person will accept to induce him to bear with it.

As for the one behavioral assumption, usually referred to as "the downward-sloping demand curve," it simply states that in response to a reduction in the price of a good, *ceteris paribus,* more of it will be demanded. In this case, the *ceteris paribus* clause includes the requirement that both the aggregate income and its distribution in the economy remain unchanged, that the prices of all other goods also remain unchanged and, of course, that people's tastes remain unaltered.[1]

It is as well to mention, however, that even though the constancies required by the *ceteris paribus* clause are not met, it is quite likely that a fall in the price of a good would increase the amount of it demanded.

In addition, there are two related shorthand terms used by economists that the reader should bear in mind. A change in the economy that results in an increase in aggregate income is referred to as an "economic improvement." Although the term "economic improvement" does indeed suggest that it is also desirable, economics regarded as a positive science has no truck with such emotive connotations. Put otherwise, there is a definitional convenience in referring to a position II whose aggregate income exceeds that of a position I, as being *better* for the economy than the I position, and to fortify such definition by the argument that, although some people may be worse off in II than in I, a *hypothetical* redistribution of the aggregate income in II could indeed make everyone in the economy better off in the II position that in the I. In sum, II is a *potentially* better position for everyone compared with I.

---

[1]In an exposition of the economic effects of immigration (as in Fallacy 2) the *ceteris paribus* clause will also hold constant the indigenous population in the host country. Any assessment of the economic effects of migration must obviously take account also of numbers emigrating, for what matters to the host country is excess immigration or net immigration. Since in the case of the United States, at least, the excess of immigrants over emigrants during the postwar years has been of such a magnitude that the analysis would have been equally relevant to the U.S. experience if conducted instead in terms only of excess immigration.

The term "economic efficiency" follows the same interpretation, being measured in terms of aggregate value (the total amount of each good consumed in the economy *multiplied* by its corresponding price). Hence if the economist states that economic efficiency is increased if a certain condition is met, no more is to be understood than a statement that the value of all the goods consumed in the economy will be greater if that condition is met.

From these shorthand or definitional terms, however, it does not follow that the economist is unconcerned about regressive distributional effects that may occur in consequence of the economy's becoming more efficient. He should certainly mention any significant distributional effects, assuming he foresees them, arising from any economic change under consideration. But the economist *qua* economist has no remit to rank one distribution of income over another: there can be no *economic* criterion for ranking income distributions. To be sure, there is a common presumption in Western societies in favor of a more equal or egalitarian distribution of income. But the determination of an ideal distribution, or even just a better distribution than the existing one, is ultimately a moral issue, not an economic one.

Finally it has to be impressed on the reader that I have restricted myself in the following chapters to judgements of *fact* (whether true or not) from which no *value* judgements may be drawn. As the saying goes: from descriptive statements one cannot derive prescriptive statements. Hence, from the conclusion that large-scale immigration acts to reduce per capita real income in the host country, one may not properly conclude that immigration into Britain should be restricted. Notwithstanding our acceptance of the fact that immigration acts to reduce per capita real income, we may still favor immigration for moral reasons: one may well argue that those born in a Western affluent society are no more deserving than those less fortunate people who, through no fault of their own, happen to be born in a poor country. Or we may favor the arrival of immigrants to our shores in the belief that a multi-racial, multi-cultural society is a good thing in itself, or that diversity is a source of inspiration, animation, and joy.

The above comments being so patently obvious, it is with more sorrow than anger one discovers that intelligent people continue to succumb to the "politically correct" view, that immigration into Britain confers *economic* benefits on its people—presumably people are anxious to be counted as being among the enlightened, or fear being dubbed a bigot or racist.

In this connection, a revealing instance is the response to a question put to the panel of four eminent persons on the BBC Radio 4's "Any Questions" program for December 14, 2007. Three out of the four panelists did not hesitate to aver that immigrants into Britain were of economic benefit to the country.[2]

---

[2]Moreover, the fourth person did not seek to contradict the others but confined himself to the point that Britain was in fact already the most densely populated of all the large industrial countries.

For the record, it should be added that among the many fallacious allegations about the benefits to be secured by immigration, there are several that also offer a sort of snapshot explanation of why this must be so. Although each of these "explanatory" allegations are palpably absurd, or at least disingenuous,[3] the palm has to be given to those who would have us measure the magnitude of the alleged economic benefits of immigrants by, for example, their "contribution to the British economy" (that is, by the sum of all incomes earned by immigrants currently residing in Britain)[4]—a proposal that for sheer breathtaking fatuity qualifies it for entry into *The Guinness Book of Records.*

I have taken the liberty of including in this volume the introductory note which appeared earlier in my *Twenty-One Popular Economic Fallacies;* a note written by the late Kurt Klappholz, a former colleague and close friend of mine during our tenure at The London School of Economics. Although always a cautious and fastidious thinker, his exemplary lucidity in expounding the methodology of economics—in effect, "the rules of the game" in economic analysis—will, I am sure, continue to delight the reader. Indeed, should he not find time to read anything else in this volume, the reader will yet agree that it was well worth buying.

---

[3]Other inane pronouncements include: (i) that immigrants bring in "new blood" that revitalizes the economy, (ii) that immigrants contribute to the financial support of the growing proportion of old-age pensioners in Britain, and (iii) that immigrant labor is necessary in order to undertake the "dirty work" or low-grade jobs that the indigenous population refuses to do.

[4]See Fallacy 2, note 5.

A NOTE ON
METHOD IN ECONOMICS

Kurt Klappholz

I

In the following pages Dr. Mishan endeavors to show that a number of widely held views on economic problems are fallacious. According to *The Concise Oxford Dictionary* a fallacy is a "misleading argument, sophism, flaw that vitiates, syllogism . . . delusion, error." Thus, in one sense at least, "fallacy" refers to logical errors. Indeed, in many of his attempts to expose the fallaciousness of certain views, Dr. Mishan concentrates heavily on their logical flaws. For example, Dr. Mishan points out that, if they are to be *consistent,* proponents of the view that an increase in the national debt imposes a "burden" on future generations would also have to argue that any failure of the government to increase the current rate of investment similarly imposes a "burden" on future generations. Yet this does not appear to be their view; hence they would seem to be inconsistent—and consistency is a matter of logic.

For an argument to be acceptable it must be free from logical errors. Logical errors are comparatively easy to discover, yet their absence does not guarantee the truth of an argument. For example, from the two premises:

    a. "All men are immortal"
    b. "John is a man"

it follows that

    c. "John is immortal."

The logic in this example is unimpeachable, but both the major premise and the conclusion are false. Many, if not most, debates in economics relate to the truth or falsity of certain propositions which may be the premises or conclusions of an argument. Examples of such propositions are "An increase in income-tax rates reduces incentives to work"; "Devaluation improves the balance of pay-ments"; "Incomes policy is effective in stopping or reducing inflation." Whether or not these propositions are true cannot be decided by logic alone and, if they are false, they are also fallacious. We must therefore turn to the question of how to decide what is true or false in economics.

II

It is, of course, notorious that economists and politicians hold different views on a number of topical issues. Indeed, one might argue that the differences between party political platforms derive at least partly from different views concerning the consequences of particular economic policies. Thus the old question arises: why should disagreement on such strictly scientific problems persist? Political parties continue to disagree about the specific *factual* consequences of high taxes, "planning," reductions in tariffs, etc. They do not similarly disagree —indeed, as political parties they have no views at all—on analogous problems in physics or chemistry (no political party has yet announced that, in its view, a man can fly by flapping his arms!). Why, then, is there so much disagreement regarding the predicted consequences of taking particular actions in the domain of any of the social sciences? Some people would answer that the reason for this is that the kind of propositions listed above are simply not scientific; that whether one believes them to be true or false depends on one's "ideology" or "values." Since different people have different "ideologies" or "values," they can never agree on the truth of such statements. This view is mistaken, despite frequent assertions to the contrary. Clearly the question "How does the levy of a tax on the development value of land affect its market price?" is on all fours with any other question regarding the effects of a particular experiment.

As is well known, natural scientists try to answer questions about the working of the universe by performing an experiment and observing whether or not its outcome conforms with their predictions. Thus, over time, disagreements are resolved and attention is turned to new problems. It is generally agreed that there is no substitute for this method of resolving scientific problems. If such questions as "Is full employment compatible with stable prices?" or "Does capital punishment act as a deterrent to murder?" are to be answered satisfactorily, it is necessary that we check our predictions about the effect of full employment on prices, or of capital punishment on murder, against appropriate observations.

One reason disagreements tend to persist among economists is the difficulty of conducting controlled experiments in economics. The difficulty may be put as follows: predictions deduced from economic theories are, in general, subject to the "all-other-things-equal" clause. Thus, when considering the effects of a tax on the development value of land, we usually abstract from other changes, for example, population growth, inflation, or changes in building techniques, which may also affect the price of land. Scientists performing an experiment, say, to investigate the behavior of bodies in a "free fall," can do much to exclude the disturbing influence of atmospheric pressure; economists cannot similarly exclude the effects of technological change. One must not, however, exaggerate the difference between the natural and social sciences in this respect. The inability to keep "other things equal" would not, in itself, be a serious source of difficulty provided we knew (a) how the "other things" changed, and (b) how such changes affect the things in which we are interested. For example, suppose we predict that the levying of a development tax will, by itself, have no effect on the price of land but it so happens that, simultaneously with the imposition of tax, there is a change in the price of wheat. If we knew how this change would affect the price of land, we could make allowance for it in predicting the effects of the tax. Usually, however, we do not have this knowledge, and we cannot then make a prediction that takes into account the change in the price of wheat. This helps to explain why the *thought experiment* has been so prominent in economics, and will show up frequently in the following chapters. It must be stressed once again that the "thought experiment," which consists of tracing the logical consequences of certain assumptions regarding individuals' behavior, is no substitute for the checking of conclusions against observations; as was illustrated above, flawless logic is no guarantee of truthful conclusions. There is, notwithstanding, some advantage in arriving at one's conclusions by a coherent argument, in particular when considering the logical consequences of different assumptions, as this is one way by which fallacies can be exposed.

III

It is perhaps fair to say that most people are interested in economics only, or largely, because of its bearing on governmental policies. So far, disputes about policies have been ascribed to disagreements about their expected consequences. It may be argued, however, that disagreements about policies would persist even if there were complete agreement about their expected factual consequences. This is so for the simple reason that most policies will affect differently different groups of people. American farmers might, for example, be in complete agreement with city dwellers about the expected consequences of the abolition of farm price supports; but this would not necessarily lead farmers to support their abolition. However, no "interest group" will openly proclaim that it is in favor of a policy which will benefit it at the expense of other members of the community! Instead, it will produce "sound economic arguments" to the effect that its interests, and the public interest, coincide. Since we know that the interests of different groups often conflict, the use of this ploy by each inevitably arouses suspicion about the "soundness" of the arguments employed. In these circumstances one may be forgiven for reaching the conclusion that the economic analysis which apparently forms part of such specious arguments is itself no more than special pleading.

Granted that economic arguments are often used to lend support to conflicting policies, must we conclude that economics is little more than the rationalization of particular interests? Such a conclusion, would, of course, be unwarranted, since any argument that can be used can also be abused. But it is as well to consider whether, and in what way, differences in material interests or in ideologies may influence the conclusions of an economic argument.

One important point needs to be made immediately. I just spoke of people using economic arguments to support the case for certain policies. If by "economic arguments" we mean—as is usually meant—statements about the expected factual consequences of certain policies, then, *from these arguments alone,* no case for or against any policy can be made. As philosophers say, from what *is,* nothing whatever follows (logically) about what *ought* to be. As far as I know, most economists accept this philosophic position. However, if this were all that could be said about the relationship between economics and economic policy, our discussion would have to end at this point with a very simple observation: economics tells us what is—or, more correctly, *what we think is*—the case; from what is, nothing whatever follows about what ought to be done. Since economics, as such, tells us nothing about what ought to be done, it cannot be said to harbor any ideological biases.

This view is much too simple-minded, however, and we may usefully consider, in a general way, how a person's "ideology" may influence his economic arguments.

Let us quickly dispose of a point which is exemplified in Dr. Mishan's discussion of the alleged "burden" of the national debt. The point is this: economists often use words in a technical sense which, in everyday language, have strongly emotive connotations. For example, economists define "efficiency" in a technical sense and, on the basis of this definition, often come to the conclusion that monopoly, or restrictive practices, or tariffs, lead to "inefficiency." As we have just argued, from such conclusions it simply *does not follow* that monopoly or restrictive practices or tariffs are undesirable. But the public at large, overlooking this point, tends to regard "efficiency" as something which *ought* to be promoted, "burdens" as something which *ought* to be avoided, and so on. Hence it is often argued that, despite protestations to the contrary, economics does tell us what we ought to do, and hence is clearly ideological. Preceding remarks sought to show that this view rests on a logical error, although it may be admitted that it would be better if economists tried to purge their vocabulary of its more emotive terms. Even so, it must be stressed that the presence of emotive terminology need not bamboozle anyone. If some economist proclaims that "full employment, inflation, and tariffs lead to inefficiency," and the listener is tentatively in favor of all three, all he need do is to ask our hypothetical economist to explain more clearly what he means by "inefficiency." The listener can then decide whether "inefficiency" in *that sense* is something he wishes to avoid.

A concrete example will easily show that the use of emotive terms need in no way inhibit critical discussions. In the United States, the term "socialist" carries strong emotive overtones—what is "socialist" tends to be regarded as bad. Many people in the U.S. object to proposals for some kind of National Health Service on the ground that it would be "socialist" and hence incompatible with the American way of life. If someone raises such an objection, we could ask him what he means by "socialist" in this context; the answer would have to be that "socialist" means that medical services would be provided to consumers free of charge, or at any rate at a price below cost, the subsidy required being financed out of taxation. If that is so, then the American pre-university educational system is also clearly "socialist," even though it is regarded as very much a part of the American way of life. Thus, assuming our hypothetical critic approves of the American educational system, we could immediately tell him that his objection to some kind of National Health Service cannot be solely that it would be "socialist." If he remains opposed to state subsidization of medical care, he has to provide other arguments.

IV

We may now turn to examples in which a person's ideology may influence the form of his argument. These examples hinge on the "other-things-equal" clause.

A classic example is the way the notion of "causes" is sometimes employed. How often have we heard it said that "*the* cause of inflation is excessive government expenditure," or "*the* cause of the U.S. balance-of-payments deficit is military expenditure abroad"? How may someone who, for example, is against inflation but in favor of high government expenditure counter such views? Or must he give up either his support for the latter or his opposition to the former?

First, it should be understood that even if there were a single or main cause, it does not follow that the single or main remedy is the removal of that cause. Indeed, a knowledge of "causes" is not always necessary, or even relevant, in proposing a remedy. To take a trivial example: if we are told that the cause of a man's destitution is the loss of his arms, which renders him unfit for work, it does not follow that the *only* remedy is the restoration of his arms. More generally, whenever we are confronted with a situation which we wish to remedy, say, poverty, inflation, a balance-of-payments deficit, the relevant question is not, "What is the cause of the situation?" but rather, "What are the alternative ways of dealing with it?" Of course, if there is only one way of remedying a situation there is little to be said; but this is not generally the case in the kind of problems with which economics deals.

To revert to our example that government expenditure is *the* cause of inflation, consider the following. While a reduction in government expenditure is one way of mitigating inflation, no one would seriously suggest that it is the only way. What, then, can be meant by saying that government expenditure is *the* cause of inflation? One sense is that mentioned above in connection with the man who suddenly becomes destitute as a result of losing his arms: until, say, last month, there was no inflation, then the government increased its expenditure, thus increasing demand in the economy and setting off an inflationary movement. This is clear enough, but it in no way suggests that government expenditure should be reduced in order to halt the inflation, unless (a) this is the only way of achieving that aim (which we regard as overriding all other aims)—and we have suggested that this is hardly ever the case; or (b) government expenditure is less useful to the community than other forms of expenditure, in which case it should be cut regardless of inflation.

It remains to consider more explicitly how these considerations are relevant to the "other-things-equal" clause. What we are about to say has been implicit in the foregoing discussion.

The arguments about the "causes of unemployment" in the 1930s provide an apt example. In the context of the theories which economists had in mind,[1] it could be shown that (ignoring foreign trade), if the quantity of money in the economy were held constant, an increase in money wages over a short period of time would reduce the level of employment, and a cut in money wages would increase it. Accepting a fixed quantity of money as part of the "other things equal," it could be said that too high money wages were "the cause" of unemployment. The fixed quantity of money, however, is not a constant fixed by God or nature, but, on the contrary, can be altered by deliberate policy measures. It is held constant only as part of our mental experiment. If, instead, we allowed the quantity of money to vary, but in the new mental experiment held money wages constant, then an increase in the quantity of money would raise the level of employment, while a reduction in the quantity of money would reduce it. With this "other things equal"—in this case fixed money wages—it could be said that "the cause" of unemployment was too small a quantity of money.

Now the two ways of increasing employment, i.e., by cutting money wages or by increasing the quantity of money, will have different effects on the price level. By cutting money wages, an increase in employment would be secured with a lower price level than if the same increase in employment were brought about by an increase in the quantity of money, money wages remaining fixed. Hence, those opposed to a higher price level might be inclined to treat *the quantity of money* as among the things to be held equal, and therefore regard high wages as the culprit; those less worried by a higher price level and more worried by workers' resistance to wage cuts might be inclined to treat wages as among the things to be held equal, and regard the deficient amount of money as the culprit.

---

[1]The notion of "cause" makes sense only in the context of a theory or law; "we can never speak of cause and effect in an absolute way, but . . . [only] . . . relative to some . . . law." Cf. K. R. Popper, *The Open Society and Its Enemies,* third ed. (London: Routledge, 1952), Vol. II, 262.

Analogous remarks may be made as regards the analysis of, for example, balance-of-payments deficits: those wedded to *fixed* exchange rates and *stable* prices (and not unduly worried by unemployment) may tend to hold these things constant in their analysis and therefore tend to regard inflation as "the cause" of the deficit; *per contra* those strongly opposed to unemployment and less worried by inflation may tend to include full employment among the things to be held constant in their analysis and therefore to regard an overvalued exchange rate as "the cause" of the deficit. In all these cases a difference in values, such as in the weights to be attached to the various aims of policy, may influence the way an argument is put by affecting the choice of things to be held constant.

V

Some writers urge that in order to mitigate this "illicit" influence of "ideology," economists discussing economic policy should engage in self-analysis in order to discover which of their arguments are prompted by their political values and which by their judgements of the facts. Honesty requires that they communicate the results of this self-analysis to their audience. Such a prescription is redundant and probably impossible to fulfill. It is impossible to fulfill because one's judgment of "facts" is often colored by one's values and vice versa. If the prescription is interpreted as demanding that economists state which of their policy conclusions follow from factual premises and which from value premises, the answer again is that they follow from both. The prescription is redundant because in any discussion a person's motives are utterly irrelevant; what matters are the arguments he puts forward. The way to avoid the misleading arguments which try to derive remedies from "causes" is to remember that, when it comes to issues of policy, the problem is to make the best choice from among the courses of action open to us. If someone presents us with a number of choices, none of which we like, we should bend our minds towards finding less objectionable alternatives.

VI

Those who agree with all of Dr. Mishan's views may find this Introduction of little interest, since they will not wish to criticize him. It is therefore addressed principally to those who may disagree with some or all of his views.

The point of this Introduction is to suggest what are, and what are not, relevant disagreements or criticisms. If a reader found Dr. Mishan committing a logical error, then this would indeed be a relevant criticism; similarly, if a reader thought that some of Dr. Mishan's views on how the economy works are false, then this, too, is a most pertinent criticism (though it must always be remembered that *believing* something to be false does not imply that *it is*, in fact, false). Again, if a reader disagrees with Dr. Mishan's views on desirable policies, for example his views on rent control, he should ask himself whether he can think of alternative policies which, on balance, can be expected to have more desirable consequences. However, one cannot relevantly criticize Dr. Mishan's views on, for example, rent control, by claiming that he is merely an apologist for land-lords, or by verbal quibbles about his particular choice of words. As Dr. Mishan explains in his Preface, he hopes that his books will contribute to a more enlightened discussion of current problems of economic policy. The kind of irrelevant criticism I have just mentioned has no place in any enlightened discussion.

U.S. GOODS CANNOT COMPETE EFFECTIVELY WITH THOSE PRODUCED BY CHEAP LABOR IN COUNTRIES SUCH AS CHINA

1. Such a belief often leads to a moral stance; that we ought not to buy goods from a country where workers are "exploited" or, at least, are paid very low wages. It is of interest, therefore, to remind readers that the exact obverse of this fallacy is one that was no less popular, especially in the United States in the wake of World War II: namely, that since productivity in the U.S. was higher in the manufacture of almost every good, it would not need to import manufactured goods from any country—though it would, of course, have to import those raw materials that could not be found within its borders.

Yet by reference to a simple exercise, it is easily shown that—compared with autarky (no foreign trade whatever)—free trade can benefit all countries engaged in it, and to do so regardless of the vast differences in pay to workers or, for that matter, to capital and land. The simple exercise which follows is in fact based on an illustration contrived by David Ricardo, a distinguished early nineteenth-century economist. Ricardo made it abundantly clear that although Britain was then able to produce both wine and cloth at a lower cost than they could be produced in Portugal, both countries could gain if Britain exported cloth to Portugal while Portugal exported wine to Britain. This was possible, however, only because Britain had an advantage in producing cloth rather than wine as compared with Portugal—the reverse being (necessarily) true of Portugal. To put it otherwise, each country should specialize in the good for which it has a *comparative* advantage.

Following Ricardo, then, the simplest model conceivable is one in which we focus on only two countries, each of which produces the same two goods although, later on, such a model can be elaborated to encompass more than two countries and more than two goods. It will be easier for the reader if we call our two countries America and India, and our two goods, machines and cloth, both goods being of exactly the same type and quality. It will be convenient also if initially we ignore all costs of transport—although, obviously, the higher are such transport costs the smaller the volume of trade between the two countries.

2. In order to compare the costs of the two goods, it is necessary first to agree on the size of a unit of cloth. Let us then, arbitrarily, make a unit of cloth equal to a bale of 100 yards, though it would make no difference at all if we chose as the unit of cloth one of 10 yards or 501 yards.

We now have to ask, what is the necessary condition for gainful trade between the two countries to take place? One thing is certain: it has nothing to do with the absolute advantage in productivity of one of the two countries. America could be 10 or 50 times as productive in general when compared with India, notwithstanding which mutually beneficial trade can take place, *provided* that the *comparative* advantage in the production of the two goods is not the same in the two countries.

Thus, ignoring altogether the productivities in the two countries, let us suppose that the cost of production, in America, of both one machine and one unit of cloth is exactly $100, whereas in India the cost of producing one machine is R.2000 and of producing one unit of cloth is R.1000 (where R. stands for Rupees). Clearly the *comparative* cost of producing a machine in America is cheaper than it is in India—the reverse, the *comparative cost* of a unit of cloth being cheaper in India than in America, being necessarily true. For ready reference, these figures are tabulated below:

	America	India
One Machine	$100	R.2000
One Unit of Cloth	$100	R.1000

Looking at each of the two columns of figures in turn we can surmise that the limits of an exchange rate of the two currencies must lie between $100 = R.2000 and $100 = R.1000—or between $1 = R.20 and $1 = R.10—if mutually beneficial trade is to take place between the two countries. We may also perceive that the closer is the exchange rate to $1 = R.20 the more America gains; while the closer it is to $1 = R.10 the more India gains by exchanging cloth for machines. For ease of exposition, let us assume that the prevailing exchange rate is somewhere in the middle of these limits, say $1 = R.15.

At this assumed rate of exchange of $1 = R.15, the $100 American machine will cost R.1500 in India, which is R.500 less than it would cost to produce in India. Yet at this same rate of exchange a unit of Indian cloth, costing R.1000 in India would come to only $66.50 in America, a savings of $33.25 as compared with its cost of production of $100 in America.

Our example, therefore, confirms the proposition that provided the comparative costs of the tradable goods differ in the two countries, as can be seen by comparing the two columns in the table, mutually beneficial trade can take place—at least if transport costs are not too high.

3. We may take the economics a small step further by asking the question, Just what, in fact, determines the equilibrium rate of exchange between the Dollar and the Rupee? The answer is the comparative strength of the demand by America and by India of the imports from the other country. Starting with the prevailing equilibrium rate of exchange—that at which the value of each country's imports from the other is equal, which can also be expressed by saying that "the balance of payments" in each country is in equilibrium—if America's demand for imports of Indian cloth increased, so that at the prevailing exchange rate, say $1 = R.15, America has an excess of imports over the value of its exports, it will be accompanied initially by an excess in the demand for Rupees over the (unchanged) supply of Rupees on the currency market—which current supply of Rupees by India is equal, by definition, to India's demand for Dollars needed to pay for its imports of American machines.

This excess of American imports from India will be removed, however, without intervention by the government, by letting the currency market operate freely in order to establish a new equilibrium rate of exchange, one in which the Dollar is devalued against the Rupee, so making American imports of cloth from India more expensive when costed in Dollars.

Let us suppose that a new balance-of-payments equilibrium in both countries is reached when the devaluation of Dollars is such that the original exchange rate of R.15 = $1 falls to R.12.5 = $1. In that case the Dollar cost of a R.1000 unit of Indian cloth will rise in America from $66.50 to $80, so acting to curb America's demand for Indian cloth. On the other hand, the cost to India of a $100 American machine will fall from R.1500 to R.1250, so acting to increase India's demand for American machines. In this way balanced trade, or equilibrium, is restored.

There can, however, be official, or institutional, intervention in the currency market which prevents such variation in exchange rates so that it remains close to the original R.15 = $1. Failing protectionist measures by America—a tariff on the import of Indian cloth, or a quota system that limits the amount of cloth imported into America—the excess of American imports from India continues. We shall touch on this possibility again in the following chapter on globalization.

4. So far we have restricted ourselves to creating a simple model in order to illustrate that, granted that the comparative costs of the goods to be traded are different as between the two countries, there *can* be mutually beneficial trade between them regardless of the absolute costs in each country. Yet in order that

free trade, or some trade, succeed in actually being beneficial in each country, there are other conditions to be met. Put otherwise, tacit assumptions are necessary if we are to conclude that the trade between countries will indeed be mutually beneficial—tacit assumptions that often go unmentioned in elementary treatments of the subject.

One reason for this incompleteness of treatment is that economists, certainly pro-market economists, have confined their analysis to the economic effect on populations in the trading countries when regarded as *consumers* only—disregarding, that is, the possible negative effects of international trade when populations are also perceived to contain workers. Hence, one tacit assumption necessary to ensure net gains from trade between countries is that no significant dislocation occurs in the economies of such trading countries. This tacit assumption cannot be accepted as valid, perhaps not even plausible, bearing in mind that when a country starts to trade with others, or increases its trade with them, some of its industries have to contract since the goods they produce are now to be replaced by imports, while some export industries have to expand. But unless the workers (and the capital) are equally adept in the relevant industries, and can move costlessly from one area to another, such tacit assumption is unwarranted.

Whenever domestically produced goods are replaced by substitutes from abroad, some of the workers in those domestic industries have to be laid off. And it may take some time before they find employment again. Moreover, if and when they do find employment, the costs of movement to a new area—in emotional as well as pecuniary terms—may be high and, also, the conditions of work may be less congenial.

It follows, therefore, that when consumers in the affluent society, thoughtlessly perhaps, switch from buying a home-produced good to buying an imported substitute, their gain in welfare is likely to be small. Yet when, in consequence of a number of consumers doing the same, a worker becomes unemployed, the loss suffered by him and his family may be considerable.

To elaborate on the above reflection, the welfare value of many of the goods that are imported by a country, and therefore to some extent the welfare value of its international trade, may not be impressive. Thus, if for any reason a large proportion of the variety of goods imported become no longer available, so that consumers perforce have only the option of buying equivalent home-produced goods, the discomfort suffered may be slight and fleeting—judged, say, by the amount of money they collectively would be willing to pay in order again to have the opportunity of buying the imported goods.

It follows that as the range of internationally traded goods grows over time, adherence to a policy of free trade is likely to exact an increased cost in terms of continual dislocation and of worker anxiety. For the more affluent society becomes, the greater becomes the array of novelties, of technological all-sorts, and of expendable items in general, offered to consumers. Inevitably the choices made by consumers become more whimsical. In consequence the demand for consumer goods, both those produced at home and abroad, may change with bewildering rapidity, influenced as it is by changes in fashion, by changes in the design of products, or by prolonged advertising campaigns.

Thus, a good economic case could be made for protectionism, or at least for more protection against the import of those goods that can be regarded either as expendable luxuries or as close substitutes for home-produced goods.

Immigrant Labor Confers Economic Benefits on the Host Country

1. This is by far the most persistent of all economic fallacies. It became popular about the mid-1950s when large numbers of families, chiefly from the Caribbean, arrived in Britain. One reason for the longevity of this economic fallacy—continually recycled by the popular media—is surely the growing influence of a "politically correct" ethos that would frown today on any suggestion that, on balance, immigration into Britain is not "a good thing," socially and economically: indeed would regard it as "racist" to cast any doubt on the social and economic benefits immigrants are deemed to confer on the indigenous population of Britain.

Recourse to simple economic analysis does not, however, bear out the popular, or politically correct, view.

2. The international migration of labor and, for that matter, of capital also, originally between European countries and later, from the mid-eighteenth century on, from Europe to North and South America, continued to expand until about 1930. Really large-scale immigration, however, the so-called South-to-North movement, began in earnest only after the end of World War II.

The unprecedented scale of this South-to-North movement may be attributed almost entirely to a virtual revolution in communications and transport that was hastened by the advent of the War. Among the mass of ordinary people living in the Caribbean, in Africa, India, and South America, there came a dawning awareness of the high material standards being enjoyed by workers in the countries of the West, an awareness that spread at the same time that travel between countries had become much cheaper and, indeed, much faster. And the fact that Britain and America came to be the most favored destinations can be explained, at least in part, by the English language being spoken, even if imperfectly, by the greater proportion of the migrants.

3. Since we are to address ourselves to large-scale immigration into this country, most of it being relatively low-skilled labor, the picture that emerges will be clearer if we paint with a broad brush.

Large-scale is to be emphasized in this connection since, in Britain with a population of about 50 million in the 1950s, the immigration of a few thousand or even of a couple of hundred thousand, spread over a few years, would not produce any significant economic effect in the country at large, even though there could be perceptible distributional economic effects if such immigrants settled in one or two particular towns or cities: inasmuch, that is, as immigrant labor seeking employment in particular areas would tend to lower wages there in certain occupations, only a material transfer is involved—one between workers there and consumers of the goods they produce. For the loss borne by the lower pay of workers (following the entry of immigrant workers into the occupations in question) is balanced by the gains of those consumers who buy the goods produced in those occupations that are now reduced in price.

4. In connection with these internal economic transfers it should also be mentioned that the occasional allegation that immigrant workers—at least until they are more fully integrated into British society—happen to contribute, on average, more to central and council taxes than do indigenous workers, from which allegation it is inferred that immigrants confer a net benefit on the host country. This allegation about immigrant workers contributing more per capita than indigenous workers to the provision of public services seems *prima facie* implausible since immigrant earnings are on average lower than those of indigenous workers.

Yet even if it transpired, over some period at least, that the allegations were true, by itself it does not signify: it does not by itself entail an economic transfer from the immigrant population to the indigenous British population. In order to establish the existence of such a transfer it is necessary also to calculate the per capita public expenditure on each of the two populations so as to enable us to compare their *net* contributions, positive or negative, to all the public expenditures on goods and services.

It therefore behooves us to take account also of all those additional public expenditures that are incurred solely in accommodating the inflow of immigrants: expenditures that would not have been incurred in their absence.

Included in such additional expenditures would be (a) those incurred in extending or adding to bureaucracies in the endeavor to monitor the entry and movement of immigrants whether they present themselves as migrant workers, as tourists, as students, as asylum-seekers, or even as spouses, parents, children, or other close relations of immigrants already settled in this country; (b) those incurred in additional social workers trained to assist immigrant families to settle in this country and, in cooperation with the police and other auxiliary agencies, to monitor their activities for a period, and also to guard them against exploitation and mistreatment by unscrupulous employees or gangs.

Such immigrant-induced expenditures include (c) the maintenance of an unofficial and official race-relations industry including the British race-relations watchdog CRE (Commission for Racial Equality), and (d) additional expenditure required for the training of police officers, of lawyers, and of social workers to be *au fait* with the implications of legislation enacted to prevent racial discrimination and racial abuse and, therefore, additional expenditures on the legal outlays necessary to implement such laws.

Nor should we overlook (e) the vast expenditures on salaries of hundreds of interpreters spread among the towns and cities throughout the country who are being continually called upon by the police, by law courts, and by personnel in the social services in order to enable the latter to communicate with those immigrants or asylum-seekers—both those recently arrived and those living within large immigrant communities—whose understanding of the English language is poor or virtually nonexistent. In this connection we should also include (f) a substantial increase in the costs incurred by a significant proportion of our elementary schools in which teachers have to teach children who have little or no knowledge of the English language.

Finally, the postwar immigrant population which, among other undesirable immigrants, has come to include terrorists or potential terrorists, has necessitated a disproportionate increase in expenditure on intelligence services to increase their efficacy in unearthing and, where possible, in penetrating Al Qaeda-inspired terrorist cells scattered throughout the country whose members are eager to become suicide martyrs in their Jihad against the West.

In sum, there continues to be inordinately large increases in public expenditure that are wholly attributable to the postwar-large-scale (multi-racial, multi-cultural) immigrant population; consequently, this increase in public expenditures has to be financed by a significant increase in taxation. Inasmuch as by far the larger proportion of this increase in taxation is borne by the indigenous population—more precisely, by those families and their descendants who had settled in the country prior to the massive postwar immigration—there exists a massive transfer of real income from the latter in favor of the postwar immigration population; which is of course the reverse of the allegation of members of the pro-immigration lobby.

We need not go on giving examples of other expenditures that would not have been incurred in the absence of large-scale immigration into Britain before concluding that even if it could be shown that immigrant workers pay higher taxes, on average, than indigenous workers, a more comprehensive calculation that included the range and variety of additional expenditures, such as those indicated above, which are incurred solely in response to the postwar immigration into Britain, could hardly fail to reveal that on balance the internal transfer of income is actually from the indigenous population to the immigrant population—the reverse of the occasional allegation.

To cap it all, even were such remote possibility realized—that, for some period at least, there were some transfer from the immigrant to the indigenous population—it would in no way detract from the indisputable fact that large-scale immigration acts only to diminish per capita real income in the host country's growing population (consisting of both indigenous and immigrant populations): it being understood that the movement in per capita real income is the critical measure of the economic impact on the host country of immigrant labor.

5. A *caveat* is in order before turning again to mass immigration. Although the reader may find it tedious to be reminded continually of the *ceteris paribus* (other things equal) clause, it is a matter of prudence to tacitly invoke it when necessary by stating that the change under consideration *acts* to produce the economic effect claimed. Thus, if it is affirmed that large-scale immigration from a poor to a prosperous county acts to lower the average real income in the host country, it is to be understood by the reader that it does so provided that the capital stock remains unchanged, that no technological progress takes place over the relevant period, and so on.

If, for example, the immigrant inflow into the host country over a two-year period were calculated to lower its average real income (*per capita* real income) by three percent, yet over the same period the *observed* decline in average real income might be only about one percent. From the true statement that the immigrant inflow in question acts to lower average real income in the host country by three percent, we are to conclude that, regardless of what the average real income of the host country turns out to be, it would yet be three percent higher than it is if, instead, no migration whatever occurred.

6. A basic axiom of economics, one of particular relevance to large-scale immigration, is that the greater the ratio of capital to labor, the higher the average productivity of labor, and also the higher the average real income.[1] Since the

---

[1]This footnote may be disregarded by the reader without having, in any way, to qualify the conclusions. It may be of interest to some, however, to know of the relationships between *average* product, *marginal* product, and *per capita* real income, even without explanation. (For an elementary student of economics, the explanations are quite simple, especially with the aid of a simple diagram, since he already has some theoretical background. In the absence of such basic constructs, an explanation of the relevant concepts would take up too much space to make it worthwhile. The inquisitive reader without such economic background will have to take the following on trust.)

Since the number of income earners in the economy (which includes landlords and shareholders) exceeds the number of laborers, the average real income, or per capita real income, must be less than the average product of labor—bearing in mind that the *total* output of the economy is equal to the average product of labor multiplied by the number of laborers.

As for the average real wage, it is determined (at least in a competitive economy) *not* by the average but by the *marginal* product of labor which, when the average product of labor is diminishing, is below the average product for any given number of laborers.

It can also be shown that the total return to the owners of capital is equal to the difference between the average and the marginal product of labor when such difference is multiplied by the number of laborers employed.

converse is equally valid, it follows that, beginning with a given stock of capital (of industrial plant and machinery[2]), an increase in the number of laborers acts to diminish the average productivity of labor, and the average real income.

Should the reader have any doubt about the validity of this basic axiom, let him assume, instead, that with the existing stock of capital, the average product of labor does *not* diminish as additional labor is employed, but in fact remains constant. It would then follow that if two countries, say Britain and India, both had exactly the same stock of capital, say £200 billion, the average product of labor would be the same in both countries even though the labor force in India were 20 times that in Britain (which would imply that the capital-labor ratio in Britain were 20 times as great as that in India). Since the average product of labor would remain the same in India as in Britain, so also would the per capita real income in the two countries. Indeed, no matter how fast the population in India expanded, its per capita real income would remain the same, and equal to that in Britain.[3]

Since nobody with any knowledge of the world can accept as true the above implications of assuming constant returns to labor, we are constrained to accept as valid that average productivity of labor does indeed diminish as additional laborers are employed and, therefore, to accept also the basic axiom, that the higher the capital-labor ratio, the higher the average product of labor, and also the higher per capita real income.

7. In order to impress on the reader's mind the economic consequences of large-scale immigration, we shall work with an extreme example. Again, therefore we restrict ourselves to two countries called Britain and India in which the population of the latter is about 20 times as great as the former. Prior to any migration between the two countries we shall also suppose that the capital-labor ratio in India is such that the average wage in India is about one-tenth that in Britain.

We may now imagine that the British people have become so big-hearted that they decide to remove all barriers to immigrants from India. Aware as the Indian people are of the enormous disparity in wages in Britain compared with those in India, Indian families begin to move *en masse* to Britain. Allowing, for argument's sake, that the costs of movement to Britain did not act as a deterrent,[4] this migration of people from India would continue until there were no material

_____

[2]It is generally understood also, at least by economists, that the stock of capital will include the investment over the past in the training of workers in order to raise their skills.

[3]*A fortiori,* if we went further, and assumed that average productivity of labor *increased* as additional labor were employed, it would follow that, even though India had no more capital than Britain, its standard of living would be higher.

[4]Migrant families from India would be somewhat fewer than the number that would equalize wages in the two countries once costs of movement were taken into account. Such costs would not only include pecuniary outlays but also psychic costs—distress at having to part from relations, friends, and from a familiar environment and culture.

advantage in doing so; until, that is, there were no difference in wages as between the two countries.

However, since the original size of the Indian population was taken to be 20 times as great as the original British population, the wage-rate that would be common to both countries once migration had ceased would be much closer to the original low wage-rate in India than to the original high wage-rate in Britain. We may therefore confidently conclude that an unimpeded migration of Indian people into Britain would substantially reduce the wages of indigenous British workers.[5]

8. It has to be acknowledged, however, that inasmuch as immigrants into Britain save a proportion of their incomes, which savings we assume are invested so as to increase the stock of capital, they will also be making a contribution— along with the annual savings of the indigenous population—to the eventual recovery of the original capital-labor ratio, and therefore to a realization of the original (pre-immigration) real wage-rates in Britain.

Yet, eventually, (assuming mass immigration comes to an end) the pre-immigration real income per capita in Britain would be restored and, indeed, therefore would grow; in any future year it would always be below the level that it would have reached in *the absence* of immigration. Nor may we suppose that this recovery of the original (pre-immigrant) capital-labor ratio will soon be accomplished once large-scale immigration ceases. The propensity to save, at least in Western countries, is seldom above five percent per annum. Allowing that after this immigration, the population of Britain has increased twentyfold, with a five percent propensity to save it would take about 100 years before the original pre-immigration capital-labor ratio of five to one could be restored.

9. As every student of economics soon learns, and as Adam Smith made abundantly clear over 200 years ago, the singular merit of a market economy is that, without any state direction whatever, it operates spontaneously and effectively —through the movement of prices of goods and also of labor and capital—to so allocate and reallocate the resources of the economy as to meet the continually changing conditions of demand and supply. Thus, whenever at the prevailing price, the amount demanded of a good exceeds its current output, the price of that good tends to rise, as also does the price of labor needed in its production. In consequence, labor is attracted to move into the production of more of this good. Moreover, since a shift of consumer demand in favor of the aforementioned good is apt to entail a shift of demand away from some other good(s), so causing a decline in prices and wages there, the redundant labor elsewhere

---

[5]Needless to point out, since the income of every additional worker settling in Britain adds a mite to Britain's GNP (gross national product), the eventual employment in Britain of several hundred million Indian workers would massively augment Britain's GNP—hence a massive "contribution" to Britain's economy.

has an added incentive to move into the production of the good that has now to be expanded in response to consumer demand.

In fact, it is only during the postwar years that Britain and other countries in the West began, unwittingly perhaps, to by-pass the familiar functioning of the market economy. Rather than giving scope for the market to function—in particular, to allow the apparent shortage of personnel in one or other occupations to actuate a rise in pay sufficient to attract additional workers, elsewhere in the economy, to move into such occupations—it had recourse instead into "importing" workers from abroad. Such action, incidentally, must have conveyed to the layman that an incipient shortage of labor in any occupation was economically to be replenished only by immigrant labor.

Clearly, the consequence of by-passing the domestic market economy in this way is that the increase in pay that would else have been actuated by the domestic economy does not in fact occur. And so, without any increase in pay, the vacancies in these occupations were instead filled by immigrant workers from low-wage countries who were, of course, willing enough to move into Britain.

Thus, by simply forestalling the operation of a domestic market, and having recourse instead to adding to our immigrant population, we were able also to forestall any market-induced rise in pay in any occupation in which there was an apparent shortage of personnel.[6] There can be no doubt, incidentally, that business organizations are fully aware that domestic wages can be held in check by drawing unreservedly on the limitless availability of immigrant labor, particularly when shortages in the provision of certain goods begin to surface.

To be sure, whenever there is a shortage of highly skilled or professional personnel, more time is involved in the training of additional personnel from the indigenous population.[7] Yet this fact of economic life cannot be supposed to impose much hardship in an already affluent society such as Britain.

---

[6]It follows that the oft-voiced allegation in Britain that "this country does indeed need immigrant workers since without them the NHS (National Health Service), and other organizations, would simply be unable to function" is palpably false.

No one will deny that if a large proportion of the personnel in any important occupation—be they immigrant workers or indigenous workers—were to leave or be dismissed, it would be most disruptive. Much time and expense would be necessary to replace them. But from this obvious fact one cannot infer that the NHS, if initially suffering from a shortage of nurses and other hospital workers, had to be staffed, solely or largely, by immigrants. For we do have a choice.

And if therefore we *choose* to become dependent on immigrant personnel rather than on our own indigenous personnel for the provision of services to the NHS, or other large organizations, as indeed we continue to, then we can hardly be surprised when we discover that we have *in fact* come to depend on immigrant labor for such services.

[7]When the alternative of "importing" highly skilled and professional workers is adopted, there can be occasional doubts about the qualifications they bring. In the case of medical doctors, for instance, we cannot be certain that, in *all* respects, they can adequately substitute for doctors who are trained in Britain.

10. Without in any way modifying the above conclusions, it behooves us to acknowledge that the preceding brief account of the operation of a market economy has now to be qualified in consideration of postwar developments.

Owing to what sociologist Daniel Bell has called "The Revolution of Rising Expectations" in the West, there has been a growing militancy there among workers, whether organized or not. It has become common enough in Britain today for workers to threaten to strike—or, to use the accepted euphemism, "to take industrial action"—if it proves no longer profitable to maintain a particular factory in its current vicinity, or even if its workforce has to be reduced owing to a failing demand for its products.

As distinct from the pre-nineteenth century years then, wages and prices are now seldom reduced even when the demand for certain products or services are suffering a secular decline. It follows, therefore, that the burden of allocating resources via the operation of a domestic market has to be borne almost entirely (were it allowed to operate) only by pay rises whenever shortages occur. Insofar, then, as foreign workers are *not* recruited or allowed to enter the country whenever a shortage emerges—wages and prices may be expected to rise so as to attract resources into the occupations experiencing shortages.

This asymmetric functioning of the market economy, where it is allowed to function, will therefore contribute in some degree to the postwar upward drift of wages and salaries that is in fact a feature of all the Western countries since World War II.[8] The resulting annual rates of inflation, however, have so far remained within tolerable limits. Whatever variation there has been may in part be attributed to variations in the proportion of the country's workforce that is unemployed—a subject treated in Fallacy 8.

As a sort of postscript to the above, we might like to tinker with the idea that a more rational, or at least a more symmetric, recourse to migrant labor as a substitute, albeit a more disruptive one, for a well-functioning market could be implemented without any increase in the size of Britain's population. Such symmetry would require that just as we "import" labor whenever there is a shortage in one occupation, we are to "export" labor whenever there is a redundancy of workers in any other. As consumer demand continues to shift from one good to another, the level of employment will thus remain constant as labor moves

---

[8]It should be evident to the reader that any rise in wages (and therefore prices) over time that is above the increase in the productivity of labor cannot raise real wages. Thus economically unwarranted wage claims over the years have only produced inflation, albeit mild inflation. Yet even a mild inflation produces untoward effects.

For one thing, since the tax system in Britain is progressive, the Inland Revenue each year (in the absence of high unemployment) will collect an increasing proportion of the country's national income. Therefore, unless tax rates are reduced sufficiently, the economic power of the state is increased. For another, those persons or families living on fixed incomes, or on fixed money pensions, are made worse off over time as prices continue to rise.

into and out of this country in response, respectively, to emerging shortages and corresponding redundancies.

In this way there will be no unnecessary growth in the country's population although, of course, its racial composition will alter over time.

11. We have, finally, to bring into the broad picture two other economic consequences of large-scale immigration.

The first arises from the fact that a proportion of our total national income is spent on imports of finished goods, components, and raw materials. Since in Britain this proportion is quite large, the increase in its population through immigration will significantly increase the volume and value of its imports.[9] Since an increase in imports worsens the country's balance of payments, acting as it does to create an excess of imports over exports, action taken subsequently to restore the balance of payments must turn the so-called terms of trade against Britain: in other words, the prices of the goods it imports (and of domestic goods that are produced with imported materials) will increase following the required devaluation of Sterling in terms of other currencies. (If we let Rupees stand for all other currencies, then a devaluation of Sterling from £1 = R.12, to £1 = R.8, would result in imports into Britain costing 50 percent more.)

More important than the immigrant-induced worsening of the terms of trade that directly raises the cost of living, is the economic effect of immigration on the given amount of land available in the host country. In general, immigration must add to the demand for building land for homes, offices, and factories, which unavoidably raises their prices so, again, reducing the country's per capita real income. In a country with a high population density, such as that in Britain, such a rise in the price of building land cannot be supposed negligible.

What is more, any increase in Britain's already high-density population, arising in the main from the settlement there of millions of immigrant families, also increases the pressure on the country's limited environmental resources, adding also to the existing pollution and the traffic congestion both within and between towns and cities.

12. By extending our conclusions from a simple two-country model to the postwar South-to-North movement—that is, to the massive migrations, legal and illegal, from low-wage countries to the relatively high-wage affluent countries of the West—we are bound to conclude that, unless such migrations can

---

[9]There is, however, no direct increase in a country's exports when its income increases. Only a somewhat tenuous and anaemic relationship may be traced.

Inasmuch as an increase of imports into Britain entails a corresponding increase, a *proportion* of this increase in income in each of these countries will in turn be spent on exports. And of this increase in the exports of each country some *proportion* will be spent on British goods.

Although, when worked out, the anticipated income-induced exports from Britain are unlikely to be significant, they can always be subtracted from the relatively substantial increase in Britain's income-induced imports (so as to yield a figure for a *net* increase of imports into Britain for any increase of its income) whether generated wholly or in part by immigrants.

somehow be curbed in the near future, it remains an open question whether acceptable levels of employment among the indigenous populations of such countries can be maintained without some decline in their real wages.

Expressing our conclusions differently, although it may be affirmed with confidence that per capita real income in all Western countries would be higher today than they actually are had such South-to-North movement of peoples *not* occurred, we can no longer be sure that, notwithstanding anticipations of a continuation of technological progress, the indigenous populations of the West can expect to enjoy rising material standards over the foreseeable future if such large-scale migration continues.

13. An addendum to our conclusions may be thought apropos by those also concerned with the quality of life in countries of the West. Not surprisingly, once policies aimed at restricting the inflow of immigrants were enacted, facilities for the forging of documents, especially for the forging of passports, improved and expanded. Even more so did criminal organizations that became engrossed with the smuggling of these Third World people desperate to get a toehold within an affluent Western country.

People smuggling has thus become more profitable yet than the smuggling of illegal drugs. Already a large and growing population of the immigrant population that has settled in Britain and America since the end of World War II is illegal. Unfortunately, illegal immigrants have difficulty in finding secure and well-paid employment. Worse, they are often in debt to, and therefore also prone to blackmail by, the criminal gangs that succeeded in smuggling them into the country. Such illegal immigrants tend to swell the ranks of those who have to work in unsavory occupations simply in order to survive. Many become denizens of the "black economy" or earn a risky living in the criminal underworld —all of which places an additional burden on our already somewhat vulnerable Western civilization.

GLOBALIZATION ACTS TO RAISE LIVING STANDARDS IN THE WEST

1. The term *globalization* is generally understood to refer to the growth in the movement of goods and peoples, of labor and capital, that began over a half century ago.

Trade between countries can be traced back to antiquity. But international trade on a significant scale did not take place until the second half of the eighteenth century, largely as a consequence of the beginnings in Britain of the so-called Industrial Revolution. As trade barriers were reduced and shipping costs declined, the momentum toward freer trade continued, encouraged in Britain by the doctrine of free trade and by the repeal of the Corn Laws in 1846.

In contrast, however, the international movement of peoples was limited, consisting, in the main, of peoples from Eastern Europe seeking asylum from persecution within the countries of the West, in particular within Britain and the United States. Only after the end of World War II, and in consequence of the revolution in communications and transport, migration on a large scale began. Being largely "economic migrants" from the poorer Third World countries to the more affluent countries of the West, this economic phenomenon may properly be regarded as a movement of labor from poor countries to rich countries. This so-called "South-to-North" movement, legal and illegal, continues to grow, being supplemented over the past decade by migrants from Eastern Europe once such countries had been admitted into the European Union.

Thus the term globalization is more comprehensive than the term international trade inasmuch as the latter term was generally understood as the international exchange of goods, whereas globalization is held to encompass also the movement of peoples, especially that of labor, and capital. The movements of labor and capital, however, are only in one direction; if that of labor can be described as the South-to-North movement, that of capital may be described as a North-to-South movement.

What concerns us here, however, is the persistent belief by the proponents of free trade that the expansion of globalization—involving as it does, not only the unimpeded freedom of goods to move between countries but also that of the "factors of production," especially that of labor and capital—must also act to confer economic benefits on all countries and, therefore, also on the countries of the West.

2. In order to assess the validity of this belief, I take the liberty of reminding the reader of the need to invoke the *ceteris paribus* clause, in particular to abstract from any technological progress. For we know that, whether globalization continues or not, continued technological innovation of itself can be depended on—in the absence of some awesome catastrophe—to raise material living standards. Again, the impact on living standards of unbridled globalization can be made more intelligible, first, by separating the goods from the productive factors (labor and capital) and, secondly, by again a licentious painting with a broad brush, at least initially.

We begin, therefore, with the simplifying assumption of only two countries as between which only two traded goods are produced in each country. Furthermore, we begin with a state of autarky in each of our notional countries, say America and India, which means that neither country has engaged in any foreign trade whatever.

We now imagine that the political readers in each country, having perused Adam Smith's *Wealth of Nation* are so persuaded, that they abolish all barriers to the import of goods from the other country. It then emerges that India exports textiles to America which, in turn, exports machines to India. It transpires that the value of India's textiles is exactly equal to the value of American exports of machines (whether valued in dollars or in Rupees)—that is to say, the balance of payments is in equilibrium—when $1 exchanges for 10 Rupees on the currency market. Both countries benefit from this free trade, America importing textiles at a cost lower than it can manufacture domestically, at the same time as India also imports machines at a cost lower than it can produce domestically. Allowing that the level of employment remains the same in each country, real income must therefore be greater in both countries.

This state of economic harmony, however, is now disturbed following a substantial investment by American businessmen in setting up a factory in India for producing miniature radio sets at a cost well below that in America, as a result of which a large proportion of the output of these radio sets are imported by

America (which necessarily reduces aggregate expenditure in America on domestic goods, so initially reducing employment there).[1]

At the existing rate of exchange of $1 equal to 10 Rupees, the total value of America's imports from India now exceeds the value of India's imports of American goods—again, regardless of whether the value is measured in dollars or Rupees.

Equilibrium in the balance of payments may later be restored only by a devaluation of dollars in which, say, $1 exchanges for only 8 Rupees, as a result of which (at the now higher dollar price of Indian goods) America reduces its imports from India, whereas (at the now lower Rupee price of American goods) India expands its imports of American goods, which so far consist only of machines.

But it is also possible that the balance of payments is not restored by a moderate devaluation of dollars in terms of Rupees. To illustrate with an extreme case, let us suppose that no matter how far the dollar declines in terms of Rupees, India will not import any more machines from America. If the dollar falls say to only 6 Rupees then, as compared with the original Rupee value of, say, ten million imported machines into India, each costing $2,000—a total value of $2 billion, or 20 billion Rupees—the ten million American machines will now cost India only 12 billion Rupees. If, at this new exchange rate, the volume of American imports of both textiles and radio sets from India is such that their Rupee value is in excess of 12 billion Rupees, a yet further devaluation of the dollar is necessary for equilibrium in the balance of payments to be restored.

In this extreme case, the rise in the dollar price of the remaining imports into America could result in claims there for higher wages to compensate for the rise in the cost of living which could initiate an incipient inflation.

3. A final sequel to the above may now be addressed.

Although an equilibrium in the balance of payments might be reached if the dollar were devalued to the extent, say, of only 5 Rupees to the dollar (assuming the devaluation does not ignite an inflation in America), the Indian government might have chosen to *prevent* any devaluation of the dollar from the original 10 Rupees to the dollar—at which rate of exchange, of course, the trade imbalance would continue, the value of Indian goods being sold to America far exceeding the value of American goods being sold to India.

How can India maintain the original exchange rate of 10 Rupees to the dollar, and so also its excess exports to America?

For the answer we have to look at the currency market, where American exporters seek to exchange their Rupees for dollars and Indian exporters seek to exchange their dollars for Rupees. Now at the original rate of exchange of 10

---

[1]If, for example, $200 million worth of Indian radio sets were imported annually into America, it necessarily follows that America's aggregate expenditure on its own goods is initially reduced each year by $200 million, so reducing income and employment there.

Rupees to the dollar, the later excess in the value of America's imports from India over its exports results in India's demand for dollars (needed for buying American goods priced in dollars) being far less in value than America's demand for Rupees (needed for buying Indian goods priced in Rupees). Since America's increased demand for Rupees has to be paid for by dollars, this *supply* of dollars is far greater than India's *demand* for dollars; it follows that India's holdings of dollars accumulates over time, being held initially as cash balances in American banks. These cash balances are, however, usually used to buy relatively short-term securities such as U.S. Treasury Bonds.

Why should the Indian government want to accumulate dollar balances? One reason is that its current excess of exports (insofar as it does not lead to inflation) acts to maintain the level of employment in India.

Another reason is that the build-up of dollar balances (or of short-term American securities) can be used at any time for buying machinery or other sophisticated items in order to expand India's industries.

There can be yet another reason for India to want to maintain its excess of exports to America which is of some interest. Once the amount of dollars held by India becomes so large that if, at any time, India sought to exchange its holdings of dollars for Rupees on the currency market, it would precipitate a sharp decline in Rupee value of dollars. The dollar price of Indian imports would rise steeply in America, which is likely to prove inflationary and could even provoke an economic crisis.

Although such a prospect may be politically gratifying to some groups in India, a marked devaluation of such dollar holdings held by India would, however, also raise the Rupee price in India of American goods, so reducing its purchasing power for American goods.

For all these reasons India might want to continue to uphold the over-valuation of the dollar, so maintaining its export surplus in trading with America.[2]

4. Our simple two-country model may quite easily be extended to represent the globalized economy of the past few decades, with "Westland" substituting for America and "Eastland" for India. In Westland we include the countries of North America (the United States and Canada) and those of West Europe (the most important being Britain, France, and Germany). Eastland will include

---

[2]One way in which India might endeavour to approach a more stable situation while maintaining its level of employment is by using its accumulation of dollar balances in America to buy shares in large companies in America or by direct investment, in America.

Such endeavors reduce the excess supply of dollars created by India's current excess of exports to America, and they also make it more costly to devalue the dollar significantly (since in order to effect a sharp devaluation of dollars India is now able to place large amounts of dollars on the currency market only by selling its shares in American industry; but it can do this at short notice only at a loss).

countries in the Caribbean, in Africa, and in Asia (in particular India and China).

One feature of the trade between Westland and Eastland is that the exchange value of the currency in some of the latter countries, China in particular, is well below its equilibrium value. Consequently such countries export to Westland goods far in excess of the value of their imports from Westland. The economic implications of this feature are, in the main, inimical to Westland.

First, the excess of exports of manufactured goods from Eastland countries necessarily displaces the production in Westland of similar goods and therefore also displaces workers once employed there in such manufactures.[3] The tacit assumption of free-market economists, that workers displaced by import of foreign manufactures will find employment elsewhere, possibly in the country's export industries, cannot be counted on, since all the unemployed Westland workers are unlikely to be so highly skilled as to be able to move into high-tech industries even if there are vacancies there. But whether or not such displaced Westland workers can be reemployed elsewhere, what is incontestable is the simple fact that a reduction in the aggregate expenditure on the domestically produced goods of any Westland country—in consequence of the rise in its expenditure on imported goods—must unavoidably act initially to reduce its level of employment.

Second, the conclusions reached in our simplified model all have their parallels in the global economy. There we find some Eastland currencies that remain undervalued which therefore result in a continued excess of Eastland exports to Westland and therefore, also, a continuing increase of some Eastland countries' large holdings of Westland's currencies which, as indicated earlier, make Westland's economies more vulnerable.

Third, the flow of capital from Westland to Eastland—which increasingly takes the form of direct investment in Eastland's manufacturing and mining capacity—while it certainly strengthens the Eastland economy, acting to raise per capita real income there, does so at the expense of the Westland economy. For were this movement of capital to Eastland somehow prevented, it would have contributed instead in raising Westland's capital-to-labor ratio, so raising per capita real income there instead.

What is more in this connection, inasmuch as the continuing inflow of capital into the Eastland economy also enables it to better train its workers and so to manufacture, with technologically advanced machinery, an increasing range of more sophisticated (electronic) items that will compete with, and eventually displace the manufacture of such items in Westland. This continuing

---

[3]The substantial excess of exported manufactures from an Eastland country such as China arises not only from its undervalued currency but also from its goods being effectively subsidized: in calculating the costs of manufactured goods, the associated "bads"—the costs of the severe environmental damage (including the damage to the health of Chinese workers and residents)—are ignored.

inflow of capital into Eastland will further create redundancies of labor in West-land—at least until such time as Westland is able to devalue its currency which, of course, increases the cost of its imports and, therefore, also the cost of living in Westland.

5. A final reflection, one that will help us to asses the economic culmination toward which globalization is tending.

As economists are aware, if all barriers to the movement of labor, or of capital, or of both, were completely removed, then their free movement would act so as to maximize world output. Such a desideratum might impress "maximizers" or justice-seekers, since the maximization of world output would necessarily also entail the equality through the world of all wages for given skills, and also equal returns to all capital (according to risk). Such a culmination would, as indicated in the preceding chapter, also act to raise the per capita income in Eastland while acting to lower it in Westland, until it was equal in all countries.

Now in fact, and in contrast to endeavors to control the inflow of migrants into Westland, there is currently very little impediment to the flow of capital from Westland to Eastland. Quite the contrary, there is a strong incentive for business organizations to invest directly in, or move their manufacturing capac-ity into, Third World countries in order to avail themselves of the abundance there of cheap labor, skilled and unskilled. This growth in the movement of capital from Westland to Eastland countries does not bode well for Westland workers.

6. Taken all in all, the reader may well come to harbor doubts about the alleged economic benefits of globalization that are to be reaped by the indige-nous populations of Western countries.

For in addition to the downward pressures on per capita real income in West-land resulting from both the large flow of migrant labor from Eastland to West-land and the reverse flow of capital from Westland to Eastland, we have to remind ourselves of some other economic implications of large-scale immigra-tion into Westland mentioned in the preceding chapter.

These include a further reduction there of per capita real income arising from an increase in the cost of imported goods and also from an increase in the cost of housing.

And to these conclusions we have to add the unavoidable reduction in envi-ronmental amenity in Westland as a growing immigrant population presses against limited environmental resources, not to mention its adding to the growth of traffic congestion and to the growth there of the ambient pollution.

COUNTRIES FORMING A COMMON MARKET REAP ECONOMIC BENEFITS

1. Two economic advantages are generally believed to follow from a number of countries coming together to form an economic union. *A* is that it creates an increase of the trade in goods between the countries joining the union. *B* is that since the common internal market is larger than the market of any one of the countries in the union, it will be able to exploit the economies of large-scale production, so reducing the production costs of particular goods. We take them up in that order.

Before doing so, however, we remind the reader of our pedagogic device of simplifying as much as possible, at least initially, prior to considering the more pertinent qualifications. In this case, therefore, we begin by supposing that no more than two countries agree to form a common market, which requires that, in respect of international trade, they act as if they were a single country. In other words, that all barriers to trade between the two countries are eliminated and also that both erect a common tariff barrier against the import of goods from all other countries.

2. Turning first to the alleged *A* benefit, we have to know something of the trade situation in each country prior to their formation of a common market. In one extreme case (a) that the two countries were both autarkic; neither of them, that is, engaged in any international trade. Clearly the formation of a common market, inasmuch as thenceforth the two countries will trade freely with each other, may be supposed beneficial—as indicated in the discussion of gains from international trade (Fallacy 1).

Again, and as pointed out also in the earlier discussion, the greater the *value* of the trade that takes place between our two countries the greater the scope for gain—the potential gain being greater the more the goods being traded are *complements* to the goods consumed by the other country, the reverse being true the more the traded goods are *substitutes*. An example of complementary trade would be the export of cattle by one country in exchange for manufactured products of the other. An example of trade in substitute goods would be the export of paints, or of cameras, by one of the countries that also imports (slightly) different paints, or cameras, from the other: for if such substitute trade ceased, not much loss would be experienced by the consumers in either country.

In the obverse extreme case (b) in which both countries had already traded freely with all other countries, neither having had any tariff barrier, the formation of a common market may be assumed to inflict an economic loss on both countries. It is, of course, virtually certain that the erection of a common tariff barrier against all other countries would act to increase the trade between our two countries. But this increase in trade between the two countries is necessarily a *diversion* of trade by each of the two countries from all other countries that, prior to the common tariff barrier, had provided them with cheaper goods. For example, if Britain imported lamb from New Zealand prior to an economic union with France, simply because it was the lowest-cost source of lamb in the world, it would no longer import lamb from New Zealand once it formed a common tariff barrier with France. For once it had to pay a high tariff on New Zealand lamb, it would be cheaper to import the more expensive lamb from France.

In this case then trade is no longer *created*, as in the preceding case (a), but it is now *diverted*—that is, diverted from the lower-cost source to the higher-cost source in the other common market country.

3. The more usual case (c) will be one in which for each of our two countries there will be both trade-creation and trade-diversion: trade-creation between our two countries, say Britain and France, since there are no longer any import restrictions between them, and trade-diversion in each of the two countries inasmuch as each will no longer import certain goods from the lowest-cost country once a common tariff wall is erected against all other countries.

Without more detailed information, therefore, one cannot determine whether, on balance, the gains from trade-creation exceed the losses from trade-diversion for each of the two countries. All one can say with confidence is that the greater the number of countries that join the common market, and the greater the *complementary* goods traded (i.e. as distinct from the trading of close *substitutes*) the greater the gain for each of the common market countries relative to the losses.

If, for instance, a group of highly industrialized countries form a common market, the growth of trade between them may be regarded in the main as trade in close substitutes—importing from one another items such as prepared foodstuffs, cameras, shoes, plastics, and so on, all of which are also produced and consumed within each of the common market countries—which does not confer much gain on such countries. On the other hand, trade-*diversion* arising from a tariff barrier *against* non-common market countries may inflict significant losses. Thus, if it were the case that all of these common market countries had, before their union, imported their meat and grain requirements from low-cost countries, which are now excluded from the newly formed common market, each of the common market countries will have to produce its own meat or grain or else import them from one or other of the common market countries—though at a significantly higher cost. Consequently although measured, say, in Sterling, the trade-creation that takes place within that common market may be large, its value may be small, possibly much smaller than the loss from trade-diversion.

What is more, the pattern of trade between a common market of industrialized countries is likely to be unstable. Inasmuch as the bulk of the goods traded are close substitutes, some alteration in price or quality in one or other of the traded goods could increase its import of them in one, or several, of the other common market countries at the expense of its own domestic production of them. The consequence for the latter countries would involve some industrial dislocation and, initially at least, some unemployment. The same might follow some successful advertising of one or more products manufactured in one of the countries, or even a spontaneous change in taste among consumers. Indeed, the wealthier a country the larger will be the proportion of its expenditure on "luxury" items, the demand for which is notably fickle, so adding to the instability of the economy.

4. Turning now to the *B* benefits that are alleged to flow from the economies of large-scale production which, it is assumed, can be provided by a large common market, there can be no doubt about its plausibility. For there can indeed be certain goods for which the lowest per unit cost of production can be attained only if the amount produced is very large. Assuming the demand is large enough to maintain the critical lowest-cost quantity, the good in question might well be produced by a single gigantic firm, in effect a monopoly in one country. Alternatively, that critical amount of the good may be produced by an industry consisting of competitive firms. Whatever the total amount being produced by each of these competitive firms—that we may assume, for convenience, to be equally efficient—is also being produced at each firm's lowest cost. Yet this lowest cost itself will decline as additional firms enter the industry.

The reason why this lowest-per-unit cost of the good, common to all the competing firms, will decline as the industry expands, and firms continue to enter, is simply because some material or component necessary to the production of that good will itself fall in price as more of it is demanded by the competing firms. For this material or component in question is supplied by a firm "outside" the industry of competing firms—this "outside" firm itself having a declining unit cost of the material or component as more of it is produced.

In either case, whether it be a single gigantic monopoly or else an industry of competing firms that is exploiting the economies of large-scale production—

even though the cost of the capital involved may run into scores of millions of Pounds or Dollars—the total workforce required to produce the lowest-cost output of the good is unlikely to exceed 50,000.

5. Before proceeding further, let me remind the reader that the "equilibrium output" of a good can be defined as that output which would be purchased at a price that is equal to its unit cost of production.

If, however, the demand for a good that is subject to these economies of large-scale production were in fact limited to the demand of the small country in which it were produced, then clearly the unit cost of the equilibrium output being produced would be well above that lowest possible cost associated with the critical output.

In general, then, the larger the market for that good, the lower the unit cost—until the market is so large that the unit cost of the equilibrium output is as low as possible. Whether, say, the U.S. market is large enough to produce an equilibrium output that attains this *lowest possible* unit cost or not, the United States may be able to produce the good at a cost that is yet lower than it is in any other country—unless or until, that is, a number of countries form a common market that is larger still than the U.S. market.

Now, if this good were to be produced only for the *internal* market of one country or for the internal common market formed by a number of countries, the palm has to go to the largest internal market.

However, once we move from the idea that the demand for the good arises only from the demand that is generated *within* the internal market to the idea of a *global* demand for that good, it becomes quite possible for even a very small country to avail itself of the economies of large-scale production so as to produce at the lowest possible unit cost.

To be sure, tariffs may yet be erected by some countries so as to preclude any imports of the good in question, notwithstanding which the imports of that good by the remaining countries may be more than large enough to maintain its large-scale production by the small country.

6. What is more, where the economies of scale are really large, the industry that is already producing that good will be difficult to dislodge so long as the global demand for that good continues.

The reason for this is best illustrated by a simple example in which it is supposed that ten million electric sewing machines annually sold are produced in Switzerland. Sold at $250, the inclusive cost of each sewing machine works out to be equal to $220—the lowest possible cost—yielding a profit of $30 on each machine sold. The running cost (or "variable cost"), which includes only the labor and material costs of producing a machine is, however, only $170, the remaining cost being the annual interest cost on the capital raised to pay for the land, plant, and machinery required. Since this interest payment works out at $50 per sewing machine, a total of $50 *times* ten million, or $500 million each year has to be paid to the bank or bond-holders, whether the plant is in operation or not. It may be inferred, therefore, that so long as the market price of this sewing machine is above $170 it is better to continue to produce the ten million sewing machines than to close down. For there will then be some net revenue above the running cost that can at least make some contribution toward the unavoidable interest payments.

If, now, some ambitious American capitalist is thinking of ousting the Swiss sewing machine industry, so capturing the world market, he will have to sustain large losses for some time on his initial investment of about $10 billion in the necessary plant and equipment. For in order to ensure that the existing Swiss industry cannot continue to produce these sewing machines, he will have to price those sewing machines he produces at a price less than, or no greater than, $170. And since the *total inclusive* cost per sewing machine he will incur if he decides to go ahead with the project will be $220, he must be prepared to lose at least $50 on each machine he sells for as many years as are necessary to force the Swiss sewing machine industry into bankruptcy. There being, however, many other opportunities available for investing the $10 billion that he is contemplating to invest in the production of sewing machines—opportunities likely to prove more profitable over a long period—he would have to be suffering from some form of monomania to invest in this venture.

If we now consider the situation in which the electric sewing machine has been patented, there is no way in which the industry can be dislodged while the patent is in effect. A quite small country, such as Singapore, might well be the only country supplying the world markets with these sewing machines if a company there bought the patent. It need have no difficulty either in raising the necessary capital, if not domestically then, say, from the London financial market or that in New York. Nor can there be any problem of staffing the plant with some 50,000 or so employees that will be required to produce each year the ten million or so sewing machines, most of which are to be exported to the different countries.

7. We are therefore compelled to conclude, first, that the trade advantages of forming a common market are far form being certain, since the amount of trade *created* within the common market may be exceeded by that lost through trade *diversion*. Even where the number of countries joining the common market is large, there can be a net loss even if the trade creation is large, yet the goods traded are in the main close substitutes for each other, rather than complementary to one another—which is tantamount to saying that if the particular goods imported from one or other of the common market countries ceased to be available the loss to consumers there would not matter much.

Second, we may conclude that a larger common market is in no way necessary to exploit the economies of large-scale production. In a global economy even a very small country may exploit these economies of large-scale production, exporting nearly all of the items in question to countries all over the world.

RENT CONTROLS ARE NECESSARY DURING A HOUSING SHORTAGE

1. It is not uncommon to read in some sections of the press that landlords in some of the more progressive cities are "exploiting" the situation by charging "exorbitant" rents or by "rack-renting" the hapless tenant. Apparently the typical landlord is an unprincipled person who readily avails himself of the urgency of other people's needs to line his pockets.

Now, as those who listen fairly regularly to "brains trust" programs must have realized, one can gain a reputation for shrewdness in a very short time merely by asking colleagues to explain the meaning of the words they use. Like most useful gambits it can be overdone. In this instance, however, we are justified in asking that the term "current housing shortage" be elucidated, for we are not likely to make sense of the behavior of landlords unless we know more precisely the nature of the situation to which they are reacting.

We might, of course, interpret a housing shortage in the light of some ideal standard: for example, "Every family of four should have, at least, three bedrooms and two living rooms with a total of not less than 11,500 cubic feet of space . . ." Such a norm sounds humane and reasonable. It might be prescribed by a conscientious social worker in the belief that it is not too far ahead of existing standards in most parts of the country. But it is obviously a very fleeting norm. A hundred years ago it would have sounded wildly extravagant. A hundred years hence, if population continues to expand, it may again sound wildly extravagant. But today there can be wide differences of opinion both as to what is desirable and as to what can be afforded.

The economist, however, can be very complacent about all this. He need not stick his neck out on so controversial an issue. Without saying a word about ideal or desirable standards he can go on to talk about a shortage of anything in a perfectly unambiguous sense. To the economist there is a shortage simply if, at the existing price, the maximum amount that people want to buy—in this case, the use of house-room—exceeds the maximum amount that sellers are willing to put on the market at that price.

It must be admitted, in passing, that it is not always easy to measure the actual excess of the quantity demanded over that being supplied. For one thing, the goods in question may not belong to a homogeneous class. Houses, for instance, may be classified into broad or fine divisions according to the problem in hand. If we want to illustrate the working of broad principles, as we do here, there is an advantage in supposing that all houses are equally desirable so far as the public is concerned. We can, at a later stage, consider what modifications of our conclusions are necessary, if any, when we remove this simplification.

There are, again, difficulties about gathering data, as well as difficulties of interpreting the facts once we have them. If, for example, we observe that the prices of all types of housing are rising and we also have information that no additional housing has been provided, we might conclude that the rise in price will lead to a diminution of the excess demand. For as prices rise, people will not be able to afford as much housing. However, from the fact that house prices rise we cannot be certain that the excess demand is being choked off. For it is possible that, just at the same time as some people are seeking to buy less housing at the higher price, other groups want to buy *more* housing, either because of increased incomes or, possibly, because of increased migration into the area. And these additions to the total demand for housing may more than offset the reduction in demand of the first group. Thus, even though there has been a rise in price, excess demand is greater than before. With these new demand conditions—those arising from migration and higher incomes—the required equilibrium price may be much higher than before.

For all that, however, the economist's *concept* of a shortage—the excess demand associated with a given price—presents no difficulty, and it is with concepts, and not their measurement, that we are concerned now.

The tendency, in the absence of government or other controls, for the price to rise when there is an excess demand at that price is a response which is taken as axiomatic by economists. It is a response which may appear to the reader as intuitively reasonable. If, however, he is loath to rely merely on intuition (for which reluctance I have nothing but praise), he can infer as much from observing the trading that is done on the floor of any stock or commodity exchange. Though the response of prices may be more tardy and erratic in less organized markets, for instance the market for secondhand cameras, the proposition is no less valid.

It may be emphasized that there is nothing automatic about this price behavior. Prices do not rise of themselves unwilled by man. They are deliberately raised either on the initiative of some of the sellers or of some of the buyers according to the custom of the market. It may thus be the literal truth that land-lords raise their rents when, at the prevailing price of houseroom, there is just not enough to go around. To that extent a fallacy does not inhere in the quoted state-ment *per se*. Nonetheless, it does attach to an implied "ought" in that statement. That is to say, there is an implication in the statement that landlords are misbe-having or breaking the rules in some sense. And it is in this implication that a misunderstanding, if not a fallacy, can be detected.

2. Let us be quite clear on this point before considering the consequences of attempting to restrain the landlords' behavior in times of a housing shortage. The reader is not being asked to acquit the landlord of greed or even of "undue" greed. He is being invited to believe that in business affairs greed is the rule and not the exception; indeed, that it is the mainspring of the market mechanism as it exists in the free enterprise systems of the West. At least as far back as Adam Smith, economists have been making the assumption that each man pursues his own interest only. No doubt there are circumstances in business when it is not politic to appear too grasping. In large organizations, moreover, frequent alterations of price lists can be highly inconvenient. But for all that, we shall not go far wrong in our interpretation of business activities if we continue to suppose that a man will sell dearer if he believes he can thereby increase his present and future profits. "Exploiting the market" or that which sounds less offensive but comes to the same thing "charging what the traffic will bear" is accepted by economists as normal business practice. However, if we cannot con-demn the reaction of landlords to a housing shortage without at the same time condemning the system of private enterprise we might yet take the view that in this particular instance a rise in the price would be unusually damaging and, therefore, that measures to inhibit the free play of the market mechanism are justified. We shall devote the remainder of this chapter to an examination of this view.

Though the material consequences of rent controls are not difficult to trace, the passions which are aroused by this inflammatory topic make it troublesome to discuss in mixed political groups, large or small. Invariably, unless the chair-man is very determined, the features of the various rent restriction Acts come under attack by some and are defended no less vehemently by others. Experience in conducting such a discussion suggests that before allowing temperatures to rise, the participants agree to abstract from any legal or political issues associated with the rent Acts and to regard the housing shortage as a commodity in short supply to which, in the first instance at least, general economic principles will apply.

If the reader suspects a retreat to an ivory tower, I assure him that he is right. It is only in this more rarefied atmosphere, untroubled by the detail and many-sidedness of earthly things, that one can gradually discern the broad features of the landscape. The reader is therefore requested to follow me into this lonely retreat and to make himself familiar with its advantages since, indeed, we shall frequently resort to it in the following pages.

Let us forget then about the differences between types of houses and imagine a rise in rents steep enough to wipe out all excess demand, in the economist's use of that term. In the "short run"—say, during the following year—we can ignore the building of additional houses, for they will be too small a proportion of the existing stock of houses to make much impact on rents. Rents during this period will therefore be above "normal"—that is, above the existing costs of providing new house-room—and this rise in the price of house-room relative to the price of all other things acts to serve notice on the community that house-room has become scarcer, and that people must economize in its use. At the higher prices, as people do economize in its use—as they agree to occupy fewer rooms and to seek no longer (at the higher prices) to occupy a larger house or apartment—the shortage (in the economist's sense) will disappear.

In the longer run, we attend to the effect on rents as the proportion of new houses coming onto the market grows. As we should expect, additional houses bring down the high price attained in the short run to the level of the normal price (which just covers costs of providing house-room), profits disappear, and there is no further incentive to increase the resulting stock of houses. We may then talk of the market for house-room as being "in equilibrium," there being no tendency for the stock of accommodation or the price of house-room to change.

A centrally planned economy faced with a housing shortage would not be criticized if it exacted economy in the use of scarce housing, and also initiated a building program to meet the current deficiency. In these respects, therefore, there is little fault to find with the repercussions of the market mechanism. Of course, if prices are not permitted to rise, we cannot expect people to further ration their consumption of house-room and the shortage will continue. Moreover, if prices do not rise, profits are not made, and businessmen are not attracted into building houses. If houses are to be built, the government then must step in and build them.

3. But, cries some impatient reader, this ivory-tower business is all very well in its way, yet what of the hardship suffered by the poor when rents are allowed to rise without limit? Let me assure the reader that a tender conscience is no necessary handicap to the economist. Not only can we admit that a rise in the price of house-room bears harder on the poor than on the rich, as of course does a rise in the price of anything that is consumed by both groups, but we can contemplate doing something to alleviate this hardship. The real issue then becomes one of the best methods of achieving this desideratum. And since it was regard to equity that prompted us to think of rent controls as a means of helping the needy, we must consider, also on grounds of equity, the following points which may be raised against rent controls.

First, it is a blunt and indiscriminating weapon. There are poor landlords and there are rich tenants; at any rate, there are many landlords (and landladies) who are poorer than their tenants. In such cases—and they are far from few since, before the First World War at least, small house property, at least in Britain, was a favorite medium for the investment of small savings—rent controls may constitute a transfer of real income from the poor to the rich.

Second, even if we supposed all landlords to be better off than their tenants, rent controls—which may be regarded as a *compulsory* subsidy from the landlord to the tenant equal to the difference between the controlled price and the estimated market price—discriminate against the owners of a particular class of property in an arbitrary manner. The discrimination is arbitrary in two ways. One, controls are applied to housing but not in general to other goods and services. Two, the controls are not symmetric. If the government also fixed *minimum* rents when rents would otherwise fall, landlords would feel less free to grumble. As it is, landlords are freely permitted to lose money in times of too much housing but are not suffered to make any during a shortage.

Nor is it satisfactory to argue that such an arbitrary procedure be accepted as part of the inevitable hazards of private enterprise along with unforeseeable changes in consumers' tastes, in technical innovations, or in the political situation. The last three are risks which the businessman tacitly accepts. He has not yet accepted government intervention of this particular sort since, according to the prevailing political philosophy of the West at least, the business of the government is to alleviate hardship or misfortune that results from the operation of natural or economic forces; to promote equity, not to create inequities.

Broad principles by which income is transferred from the community to the government both for its direct needs and for distribution among the poor have already been accepted by the community. Each contributes according to his income, and according to his expenditure, on a scale laid down each year by the government. One may, of course, protest that the tax rates are too high or the incidence too progressive, but there is general acceptance of the basic principle: from each according to his income or expenditure. The burden of any additional help to the poor should on this principle therefore be borne by the taxpayers as a whole and not made a charge on a particular body of people merely because it is administratively convenient and politically popular to compel them to bear it.

If we accept these objections to rent controls, we might go on to propose that (a) only the really poor (defined in some socially acceptable manner) qualify for low controlled rents, and (b) the difference between the estimated market rent and the government-controlled rent be paid by the government on behalf of the poor tenant to his landlord, the funds necessary to finance this subsidy coming out of the general revenues.

The letting of council houses at a rent well below the free market rent would seem to accord with these proposals. Those eligible to occupy them are working-class people and are supposed to be earning low incomes—though it is not unknown for combined family earnings to be well above the national average for families. And the subsidy is financed from the councils. Moreover, the amount of the subsidy is such as needed to make available to the ostensibly poorer families' houses or apartments at a rent well below their market rent. Nonetheless, even these more equitable arrangements are open to criticism on allocative grounds.

For one thing, if we subscribe to the doctrine that, in the choice of material goods at least, each person knows his own interest best, then it would be better to give these subsidies *direct* to the poor to spend as they wish. After all, any person will consider himself better off if he is given an annual sum of money to spend freely than if the sum is given to him contingent upon his spending it in a certain way.

For another, the subsidy which is tied to house-room has the disadvantage that those who receive it have less incentive to economize on scarce housing than they would have if, instead, they received a direct, or unconditional, subsidy. The direct subsidy, we must suppose, is calculated to enable them to rent at the higher (market) price the same amount of accommodation, if they wish it, as they enjoyed under the system of controlled rents. But many of them are more likely to choose to rent *less* accommodation if they have to pay the full market value and, therefore, to use some part of their direct subsidy in the purchase of other things. Insofar as there results from this method of direct subsidy a reduction of the rooms they occupy and, therefore, a release of additional accommodation to the rest of the community, there will be some decline in the market price of house-room.

4. So far, what we have said in connection with a housing shortage might equally well have been said in connection with a shortage of any other good or service. However, there have been several features particular to all rent-restricting legislation which are worth looking into.

(a) Not all rents were subject to controls, but only those below a certain rateable value. There was, then, a free sector of the housing market in which rents could rise without legal prohibition.

(b) In the controlled sector, rents were fixed initially with reference to their prewar level, and later on by reference to rents ruling at some earlier date. Since prices *in general* had doubled over the war period, and continued to rise over the postwar period, the level of these controlled rents, far from reflecting the relative scarcity of housing by rising somewhat higher than the general level of prices, did not rise at all, or rose only by a limited percentage permitted by subsequent legislation. In *real* terms controlled rents were a half, and later on only a third, of what they had been before the war.

(c) Many of the rents of apartments or new houses, in particular of the more expensive kind of houses or apartments, built after a certain date, were exempt from controls. This feature was clearly designed to encourage new building by private enterprise. In the event, private enterprise, not surprisingly, sought to invest in houses or apartments to be let only to the middle class and the well-to-do. It was left to the councils to provide the bulk of the new working-class accommodation.

These three features issued in several undesirable consequences. First, since there was this very large difference between controlled and uncontrolled rents, a tenant fortunate enough to come under the terms of the Act then in force knew that if he left his existing abode he would not be able to find another vacant rent-controlled house or apartment—at least not without paying a prohibitive premium, or "key money." In effect, the condition of his continuing receipt of this subsidy was that he "stay put." In the immediate postwar period when, owing to the need for readjustment to a peacetime economy, a high mobility of labor was imperative, there was this strong inducement for a large part of the working population to remain where it was.

Second, as may be gathered from our remarks on the difference between a house-tied subsidy and a direct and unconditional subsidy, the larger the controlled sector of the market—the sector in which people have no incentive to economize on scarce housing—the greater the housing shortage, and therefore the higher the level of rents paid, in the uncontrolled sector.

Third, owing to the exceedingly low level of rents in the controlled sector, landlords had little inducement to keep their premises in good condition. If there was any definite hope of their property being freed from controls in the near future, landlords might have struggled along to maintain the condition of their properties in spite of the fact that, more often than not, their return was substantially less than the current costs of depreciation and repairs. But until such assurances were forthcoming, landlords took the view that any expenditure on their property (other than that which could not be avoided) was tantamount to throwing good money after bad. In the circumstances, a vast proportion of the nation's housing was left to deteriorate rapidly at a time when there was something of a housing famine.

5. Before we summarize our findings, let us dispose of one common misapprehension: that rent controls prevent inflation. The argument runs as follows: since rents enter heavily into the cost of living, a rise in rents would lead quickly to a demand for higher wages by the unions which would raise current costs and, therefore, current prices.

If this argument were correct, there would seem to be a case in equity for holding down the prices not only of house-room but of all other things too. Rather than have landlords subsidize their product to the tune of some 50 to 75 percent, why not instead have *all* commodities and services subsidized by their producers to the extent of something between 10 and 15 percent? However this may be, the argument is weak at three points.

(a) If, in fact, all rents were allowed to rise freely, wage-earners and other people would be spending a great deal more on rents and, to that extent, less on all other goods. The additional amount they would have to spend on rents represents, of course, additional income to the landlords who could, if they chose, buy up those goods and services which the rest of the population now had to forgo. However, if the landlord class is more thrifty than the other classes in the community, in particular the wage-earning class—and this is taken to be a fact by economists—this transfer of income from the rest of the community to landlords would result, on balance, in a reduction of aggregate demand and would therefore contribute to an easing of any existing inflationary pressure.

(b) It is not to be imagined that the wage-earner is ever short of a reason for tabling a claim for increased wages. Any belief that, if deprived of this particular reason, they are unlikely to agitate for wage increases is politically naive. A good union leader will make serious attempts to wring concessions from an employer only if he believes there are good prospects. If the chances of getting a rise are known to be slight, extreme measures are not likely to be resorted to.

(c) The opportunity for raising wage-rates will depend not only on the attitude of the industry, but also it will depend on the attitude of the government through its ultimate control of the banking system. The industry may be quite prepared to grant wage increases in the belief that the increased costs can easily be passed on to the public, but if the government pursues a policy of monetary stringency, some firms first, and sooner or later all, will just not be able to pay higher wages. The banks will not be able to lend them the additional money necessary to meet higher wage bills. Indeed, the banks will be calling in their loans rather than expanding them.

6. Let us conclude; in general, a shortage of any good in the economist's sense causes its price to rise. This acts to compel people to economize in its use and at the same time makes it profitable for private enterprise to increase the supply. If, as a consequence of a steep rise in price, poorer people suffer hardship a neater and more equitable way of alleviating this is by direct cash transfers from the general revenues. The alternative policy of holding down rents leads to socially undesirable consequences. Many tenants are made better off at the expense of their poorer landlords, and landlords as a class, *instead of the community at large,* are made to subsidize a large proportion of the community's tenants. In addition, rent controls have served to reduce the mobility of labor at a time when it is believed that it needs urgently to be increased. They have discouraged private investment in working-class accommodation, and have caused rapid deterioration in the existing stock of rent-controlled housing.

We have not discussed the administrative feasibility of direct subsidies to the poor, though clearly this would have to be taken into account in any such scheme. My opinion, for what it is worth, is that the method of direct subsidies would be far less costly than the system of rent controls with which we are familiar. It would certainly entail less social friction and require none of the cumbersome legal machinery set up under the rent restriction Acts.

As for political issues, it might be urged that rent-restricting legislation is relatively easy to enact. It has more popular appeal, being commonly understood by the greater part of the electorate as a "Robin Hood" measure to help the poor.

But it will be a sad day for the community when the economist, or any scientist for that matter, takes it to be any part of his task to promote or justify a policy on the grounds that it is "practical policy." His task is to point out to the community, as clearly as he can foresee them, the material implications of the alternative policies from which it can choose. This task, if discharged honestly, will effectively inform the concerned public of the economic consequences of the more popular, if more facile, measures being proposed for dealing with some current social problem, in this way increasing the likelihood of an alternative economic policy of greater wisdom eventually prevailing.

THE FACT THAT WOMEN'S EARNINGS ARE SIGNIFICANTLY BELOW THOSE OF MEN IS EVIDENCE OF DISCRIMINATION

1. If we simply take the national average of women's earnings then no one will be surprised to discover that they are well below those of men, if only because the proportion of women workers in the lower-paid occupations far exceeds that of working men. Thus, if there were an economy with a workforce consisting of 100 men and 100 women and in which there were only two occupations, nursing which pays $400 a week and building which pays $800 a week, the earnings of both sexes would be the same if the same proportion of both men and women entered the building profession. If, however, 80 women were nurses, the remaining 20 being builders, the reverse being true of the 100 men, then the average weekly wage of women would work out at $480, that of men at $720.

This preponderance of women in many lower-paid occupations has been customary for some time. Secretaries and receptionists in business organizations are generally women, and for the most part young, as also are dentists' assistants and hospital receptionists. The secretarial staff in the clinics of general practitioners are usually women. Apparently allegations of "sexism," "lookism," "ageism" fall on deaf ears. The owner of a pub may have reason to believe that a pretty barmaid will increase his sales of beer, liquor, and snacks, when compared with an elderly woman or elderly man. Similar beliefs may affect the employment policies of restaurants in particular locations.

As for the overt deliberate discrimination between the sexes, this continues to be unquestioned in certain activities, most obviously in sporting events such as those of the Olympic Games. Such discrimination is, of course, wholly warranted inasmuch as it is acknowledged that, in general, the greater physical strength and stamina of men compared with women give them an innate advantage. This male advantage can be important in other activities such as fire fighting or face-to-face combat in war. In the former, the average woman is likely to find it more difficult than the average man in carrying an adult person down a high ladder. In the latter case, women would be at some disadvantage in hand-to-hand combat with men. Moreover, however women behave in front-line action, their presence appears to have adverse effects on the fighting abilities of the male soldiers. It has been observed, for instance, that men on the battlefield are far more disturbed by the agonized cries of wounded female soldiers than those of male soldiers.

2. Discrimination either in favor or against the employment of women that is sanctioned by custom, or else rationalized by physical performance or otherwise, however, is not an issue that excites much controversy. What does excite controversy, certainly among ardent feminists, is discrimination against the employment of women in quite ordinary jobs or, worse, their employment there at lower rates of pay.

A few words first about discrimination against the employment of women in large organizations, or about there being a preference for men employees. In response to such observations, seemingly benign legislation was enacted in the United States in order to combat what appeared to be discrimination against the employment of women and ethnic minorities in large organizations and universities. The resulting so-called Affirmative Action took the form of reserving quotas in such organizations for the employment of "protected minorities"—a term that, for legislative purposes, also encompassed women.

The predictable response in good universities that adopted Affirmative Action was to reduce the credibility and respect of those members of the faculty that were women, or blacks, or other members of a protected minority, regardless of the rating of their qualifications or ability.

Again, whether or not one favors Affirmative Action when invoked to support minority quotas for the limited places available in good universities, regardless of the ability of quota-students to benefit therefrom, such action is economically wasteful since it acts to reduce the returns to the investment in higher education.

3. The economist, although not invariably opposed to government intervention in a free enterprise economy, is always wary of such intervention even if only to point out occasionally that it is unnecessary if its purpose is to rectify an assumed anomaly. So what about the continued allegation that the pay of women is significantly below that of men in the same occupation even though the productivity of the two sexes are apparently no different?

The economist's answer is simple: such discrimination just cannot occur within the private sector of a competitive economy. He is able to show that if, by some fluke, there were indeed a significant difference in the pay of men and women engaged in the production of a particular good, it could not be maintained.[1]

Let us begin then by supposing that in any particular industry both male and female employees were in all relevant respects equally productive, yet—owing to ignorance or sheer prejudice—female employees were paid significantly less than male employees.

In this industry, therefore, the firm that happens to be employing proportionally more women than the other firms would have a competitive advantage over the other firms. Since women cost less than men, the average production costs of this firm would be lower than those of other firms and, therefore, it will be able to expand its share of the market by lowering its prices. Unless other firms follow suit they will lose business to this one firm.

However, in order to attract additional women into the industry by inducing them to leave their current occupations, such firms would have to offer higher pay. Moreover, since the additional women now entering the industry at the higher pay must necessarily be replacing men, the resulting increase in unemployed men also acts to make men more amenable to making concessions in order to hold on to their jobs—that is, to accept some reduction in pay that is at least comparable with the now-higher pay being received by women.

Thus the uninhibited operation of market forces in a competitive economy, of itself, acts to eliminate any significant differences of pay between the sexes, at least when both are equally productive.

It is as well to impress the reader's mind by assuming an extreme example in which there are but two large firms each producing widgets of the same quality. Each of them employs only men at a given wage, has the same average cost per unit widget, and enjoys about the same share of the market. One day, the manager of one of the two firms discovers that women are perfectly able to do the same job and also that they would work for 20 percent less pay. In ruthless pursuit of profit, he replaces all his workmen by women. In consequence of the substantial reduction in his costs he is now able to drive the other firm out of business—unless the other firm follows suit.

A new equilibrium in which women only are employed in the widget industry, however, is not one that is likely to occur. For, as indicated earlier, the attracting (by the higher pay) of additional women into the industry would entail the replacement of men who, in the endeavor to retain their jobs, would be likely to be willing to accept the now-higher women's pay rather than remain unemployed, even were it somewhat below their original pay.

---

[1]To be sure, if a competitive sector of the economy did not exist or was vestigial, lower rates of pay for women could be maintained even though economically unwarranted—at least unless or until political or industrial action were effective enough to equalize efficiency pay for both sexes.

Yet even if only a fraction of a country's economy were competitive it could be enough to thwart a policy of economically unwarranted discrimination within those occupations common to both the public and the private sectors of the economy.

We may reasonably conclude that the changes induced by the operation of a competitive market economy would eventually result in an equilibrium in which the same wage is being paid both to equally productive men and women employees. Indeed, it could hardly be otherwise for very long since, as indicated, if *any* significant difference in pay remained, firms employing proportionally more women, would expand at the expense of the other firms until a new equal-pay equilibrium was established.

4. So far we have addressed ourselves to the more common practice of *time*-rates of pay—payment by the week, day, or even by the hour—irrespective of the performance of the employee working at a particular task. In the production of some goods, however, employees are on *piece*-rates; that is, the employee is paid solely by the amount of the good he produces. Such a system implies that the labor cost of a unit of the good will be exactly the same regardless of the amount produced by the employee and therefore regardless also of whether the employee is male or female.

The reader may be tempted to infer that in all firms operating on piece-rates there can be no economic warrant for paying female employees less per piece than male employees; that, indeed, if lower piece-rates were paid to females, the firm could lower its costs by employing only female labor.

The possibility of this being a false inference, however, can be illustrated by a hypothetical case in which a competitive firm discovers that it can do better by paying its female employees, say, $36 for every hundred yards of fabric instead the $40 that it pays is male employees.

In order to understand why such pay discrimination can be in the firm's best interest, we need first to distinguish between the *variable* costs of production (chiefly the costs of labor and materials) and the *total* costs of production which includes both the *variable* costs and the *overhead* costs.

Overhead costs are those payments that the firm has to meet annually, or periodically, regardless of the amount of the good, if any, produced by the plant. For they consist of the annual rent of the land, or of the premises, along with the annual, or periodic, interest payment to banks and/or bond-holders on the sums borrowed by the firm to enable it to buy all the machinery and equipment necessary for the production of the goods in question.

Now, in a competitive economy the firm has to accept as a datum the prevailing market price of the good it produces, which market price will, of course, vary over time according to the vicissitudes of the market. Clearly, if the market price of the good happens to fall below the variable costs, the firm will incur losses if it produces any of the good. Provided, however, that the market price of the good is above the per unit variable cost of its production, the excess of price over variable cost is to be regarded as a contribution to the payment of the overheads: the higher the market price of the good, the larger the contribution. Indeed, the market price can be so far above the variable costs that not only can all overhead payments be met but there will be left, in addition, a net profit.

However, provided always that the market price exceeds the variable costs, the contribution made to the payment of the overheads will vary directly with the amount of the good sold at the market price, being greatest, therefore, when the plant is working at full capacity.

To illustrate, suppose there are but 25 employees working in one of the firm's weaving sheds containing 100 looms, all producing a particular fabric. Each employee operates four looms and is paid $40 for every 60 yards of fabric. Since all 100 looms will be operating in order to sell as much of this fabric as possible at the prevailing market price if, over the year, male employees produce, on average, greater amounts of the fabric than do female employees, the firm will produce more of the fabric each year if only male workers are employed—so making a greater profit, or at least a greater contribution to fixed overhead payments.

It follows that if any female operatives are to be employed, their lower outputs over the year, which result in a lower contribution to the overhead payments, can be compensated for only by reducing their piece-rates of pay. Thus, it may transpire that the firm will be indifferent to employing male or female workers only when the piece-rates of the latter are reduced to $36.

Nor need it be the case that female employees are any less efficient in operating the looms. It may simply be the case that they are generally less reliable than male employees over the year: they are more likely to quit work if they get married, occasionally require maternity leave (incurring costs of replacement), and become more irregular in attendance once they have children. If so, then over the years their outputs are less than those of male employees and, therefore, unless their piece-rates are correspondingly reduced, the firm will sell less, and so earn less.

A REDUCTION IN BUILDING COSTS WILL REDUCE HOUSE PRICES

1. It may be easier, before dissecting this fallacy, to address ourselves to a related problem, that of a tax on land.

Since a tax on a good is generally expected to raise its price, it is not surprising that people should believe that a tax on land should also raise its price. As distinct from most goods, however, land is an asset that, within a country or defined area, is fixed in supply. Whether it is used for agriculture, for grazing, for growing trees, or for building on, the available land in the country, or defined area, cannot be augmented. To be sure, although one may envisage a tax so exorbitant that the land would be left fallow, it certainly would not raise its price, or market value. It also follows that a capital gains tax on any increase in the market value of some plot of land will have no effect either on this prevailing market value.

2. It is of interest to note that the argument employed to establish this proposition can be traced back to David Ricardo, the famous early-nineteenth-century economist, when he defended landowners against the charge of raising their rents to farmers, so raising the price of corn. He was able to show that, quite contrary to the then-popular view, it was the rise in the price of scarce corn that raised the rent of land and, therefore, the market value of the land itself.[1]

3. Whether the landowner himself actually pays any tax on his land or whether, instead, it happens to be paid by someone who buys it from him, makes no difference to the outcome, so we may as well assume that it is indeed the

---

[1]Recognizing that the fertility of the land varied from one area to another, Ricardo also pointed out that, at the prevailing price of corn, the more fertile the land the higher would be its rent. It would follow that a rise in the price of corn would not only increase rents but might also bring into production "marginal" lands, hitherto left fallow.

landowner who pays any tax on his land or, indeed, any capital gains tax, should the market value of his land increase.

Allowing that a competitive market exists in each of the products for which the land is used, their corresponding market prices have to be accepted as a datum. But since we are concerned here with land to be used for building on, it will be more apropos to illustrate the argument with a homely example in which a landlord receives an official permit to use ten acres of his land, hitherto used in growing crops, for building 20 identical houses of a specific design, each such house owning one half acre of land. Rather than undertaking the building himself, we may assume that he will choose to sell the ten-acre plot to a builder.

Suppose now that, prior to receiving the building permit, the annual value of the crops that were grown on this ten-acre plot was such as to warrant a market value for the plot of $100,000. Once it became available for building the 20 houses, however, its market value shot up to $2 million, an increase in value of $1,900,000.

Clearly, this substantial rise in the market value of the land has to be attributed to the higher value of the 20 houses as compared with the value of the crops that were grown on this plot. If each of the houses can be expected to sell at $400,000, or $8 million for all 20, and the building cost of each house is $300,000 (including the builder's normal profit), a total building cost for the 20 houses of $6 million, then the builder who secures the contract can make a windfall profit of $2 million *less* whatever he has to pay for the ten-acre plot.

If there were but one builder interested in buying the plot from the landowner, some bargaining would take place between the builder and landowner. In that case, most of the windfall of $1,900,000 ($2 million less the original market value of the plot, $100,000) will accrue to the more astute bargainer. In fact, however, there will be any number of builders competing against each other for the deeds to this valuable ten-acre plot. This competitive bidding is sure to culminate in as near to $2 million as makes no difference; for any smaller sum offered by a builder will leave some bit of windfall profit which will be whittled away by the other competing builders eager to own the plot.

If the landowner has now to pay a capital gains tax on the $1,900,000 increase in the new market value of this ten-acre plot, it will make no difference to this new market value whether the tax be 40 percent or 99 percent. The landowner has to bear it himself since there is no way of passing it on: he certainly cannot raise the expected price of the 20 houses that, in the last resort, is responsible for the new market value of the plot of $2 million.

4. What emerges clearly from the above example is that a tax on the market value of a plot of land, as also a capital gains tax on an increase in its value, does not result in an increase in its market value; in fact does not change its value at all. For its prevailing market value is determined solely by the market price of the products grown or built on it. Thus if, in our example, the 20 new houses built on the ten-acre plot were later to rise in price from $400,000 to

$500,000, the sale of such a house by its owner would yield him a capital gain of $100,000, as indeed it would to all the owners of such houses should they also decide to sell at that time. This gain of $100,000 to the house owner is to be attributed to him as landowner of his half acre of land on which his house is built. Indeed, had the builder of these 20 houses waited until their market prices increased by $100,000 each, then he himself would have been able to sell this ten-acre plot for an additional $2 million (20 x $100,000), since the market value of the plot would then be equal to $4 million—$10 million being market value of 20 houses at $500,000 each *less* the $6 million cost of building them.

Such an example of a rise in the price of the 20 houses simply confirms our conclusion above—that the market value of any piece of land is determined wholly by the market price of the products grown or built on it, and will be quite unaffected by any tax (or subsidy) on it.

5. Since in the preceding sentence we have added *subsidy* in parentheses, let us elaborate briefly since another plausible fallacy is that a subsidy to a builder of houses will reduce their prices.

Let us therefore begin again with our example of a ten-acre plot on which 20 identical houses are to be built, each at a cost of $300,000 and each expected to be sold at $400,000 which, as stated earlier, will yield a market value for the plot of $2 million—this $2 million being equal to the largest sum a builder would pay for the ten-acre plot. We now suppose that the government offers a $60,000 subsidy to the builder on each of the 20 houses built, a total subsidy then of $1,200,000.

Since the builder will receive this $60,000 from the government on each house that he builds, his residual *effective* building cost for each house becomes only $240,000. As a result the market value of the plot will rise from the original $2 million (without the subsidy) to $3.2 million with the subsidy.

This follows from the proposition that, allowing that the total market value of the 20 houses to be sold by the builder remains at, say, $8 million, the most a builder will pay for the ten-acre plot—the excess of $8 million over his building costs—will vary according to the magnitude of his building costs, being therefore higher if his building costs decline. Consequently when, because of the subsidy, his effective building costs fall from $6 million to $4.8 million, the builder will be able to pay as much as $3.2 million for the ten-acre plot, which $3.2 million then becomes the market value of the plot. In sum, the government's subsidy has no effect on the market price of the houses; it serves only to increase the market value of the land.

Nor does it make any difference if, instead, the actual cost of building were to decline as a result of a newly invented automatic brick-laying machine, the cost of each of our 20 houses now being only $240,000. For, again, the total cost of building the 20 houses, having fallen from $6 million to $4.8 million, the most a builder will pay for the plot of land will rise again by $1,200,000.

6. It should be manifest that all our results necessarily follow simply from the fact that the asset in question, here building land, cannot be augmented. The same result would follow if some particular good were fixed in supply. If the annual supply of widgets were fixed at 10,000 so that, given demand conditions, they sold at $10 each, we might hazard a guess that if, instead, 15,000 were put on the market, the 15,000 could be sold only if the widget price fell to $7. But whether our guess is right or wrong will make no difference to the observation that a fixed 10,000 annual supply of widgets will sell at $10 each. Should the *cost* per unit widget fall by half, indeed if the widget cost were zero, can make no difference to the $10 per widget that consumers will pay when 10,000 widgets only are placed each year on the market—this $10 being the most a person will pay for the 10,000th widget. The remaining buyers of widgets will generally be willing to pay more than the market price of $10, this $10 being the highest price at which *exactly* 10,000 widgets can be sold.

7. Such conclusions bear directly on the popular demand in the United States for "affordable housing," bearing in mind that the real increase in house prices in America since World War II arose directly from the greater demand for houses, and therefore for building land, which greater demand itself is also attributable to the substantial increase in U.S. population. It follows that, in the absence of the larger-scale immigration and a high birthrate among immigrants, the prices of houses would be significantly lower.

Be that as it may, the existing demand for houses in the United States, or more specifically the demand for houses in particular areas, allows that no government tax or subsidy to the owners of the building land in that area can make any difference to the prices of houses to be built there. Nor, as we have argued above, will any reduction in building costs lower house prices.

In fact the only way in which the price of a house that is to be built can be made lower is either to increase the amount of building land, transferring it from agricultural land, grazing land, "brown field" land or else from the "green belt"—which itself necessarily entails an expansion of suburbia when the additional building land to be provided is that surrounding the suburbs of our towns and cities. Failing that, the government would have to subsidize directly the *buyer* of the house on existing building land.[2] Assuming the subsidy needed to make the house "affordable" be equal to $100,000 or more, a million or so of "affordable" houses will cost the Treasury as much as, or more than, $100 billion. Annual taxation in the United States would then have to increase by this $100 billion or else all, or some part of it, could be financed by reducing expenditures on pubic services during the year. In effect the subsidy would

---

[2]The $100,000 subsidy may be made direct to the house buyer himself, by some central agency which buys the house at its market price and sells it to the house buyer at $100,000 less than that, or else to the builder *conditional* upon his selling the house at $100,000 below its market price— always assuming that there are inexpensive ways of enforcing the requirement.

amount to a transfer from taxpayers to the buyers of these now "affordable" houses.

8. A brief caveat may be admitted lest a reader be so careless as to conclude from the above argument that house prices over the future cannot decline. For they will indeed decline, generally or within specific areas, should the demand for housing itself decline. This may occur as a result of a decline in income and employment in the economy at large or in some specific areas of the economy, or as a result of growing preference for caravans or mobile homes, or of prohibitive taxation on second homes, or else—and more commonly—from a gathering expectation that house prices are about to fall.

In sum, the fallacy uncovered in this chapter is the common belief that a reduction in building costs will reduce the price of houses. For the simple fact is that the prices of houses built, or to be built, on any given acreage of land, are determined wholly by the demand for those houses, that is, what people are willing to pay for them.

Fallacy 8

JOBS ARE LOST WHEN A FACTORY OR BUSINESS CLOSES DOWN, AND VICE VERSA

1. One may interpret the above as a tautology thus: if a factory closes down, then there can be no jobs there. This interpretation of the above title is, however, of no interest. It is, nonetheless, evident that the more we restrict our attention to the affected locality, the more true is the proposition that jobs are lost when the business in question closes; therefore, the *less* true—or, rather, *possibly* less true—the greater is the area of the economy considered.

If a factory that produces only one kind of camera closes in the town of Clickton, somewhere up North, the one hundred men and women employed there are obviously out of a job, at least for a while—unless, by some coincidence, it happens that a new factory producing much the same kind of camera is opening in the vicinity. If, however, a camera-producing factory of the same size is being opened instead somewhere in the South of the country, the loss of one hundred jobs in the North is offset by an addition of one hundred new jobs in the South. Indeed, where we can ignore the costs of movement of people, the one hundred workers could simply move to the South of the country so that not only does the level of employment for the country as a whole remain the same but no employee in the country would lose his job. The same could be said even if a shift occurred in consumer demand from, say, $20 million worth of a good X produced in the North to $20 million worth of a different good Y that is produced in the South, provided that workers could not only ignore all costs of movement but could also turn their hands to any job.[1]

---

[1] In order for the employment level to remain unchanged in such cases, it has to be true also that an annual expenditure of $20 million creates the same number of jobs whether in producing good X or good Y, which is not necessarily true. If in the production of Y far more capital per worker was used than in the production of X, a shift of a $20 million expenditure from good X to good Y would release more workers from producing X than would be required in producing $20 million more of Y. We shall, however, disregard this qualification in order to simplify the exposition.

In the world we live in, of course, there can be prohibitive costs of movement from one part of the country to another and skills can be very different or, if not skills, conditions of work, or the attractiveness of the available employment opportunities, can be quite different. If there is a shift in the demand for coal to, say, a particular sort of consulting service that would require additional secretarial personnel, it would be surprising if any discharged coal miner would consider applying for a position as secretary.

2. Broadly speaking, therefore, we may affirm that the level of employment in the country as a whole is directly related to its aggregate expenditure: if the latter increases by, say, ten percent, then the level of employment will increase by roughly ten percent, provided there exists unused output capacity in the economy.

It is useful in the connection to split the country's aggregate expenditure into several, though possibly related, components, beginning first with that of expenditure on consumer goods and that on investment goods, whether or not the change in either arises in the private sector or in the government sector of the economy.

With respect to aggregate *consumption expenditure,* as a proportion of aggregate income, it is generally taken to be fairly stable over a number of years unless there happen to be substantial changes in interest rates. However, it is not taken to be equal to aggregate income since most people save a proportion of their incomes, the fraction saved being referred to as "the propensity to save." Thus, if the average propensity to save for the community as a whole were 0.1, the remaining fraction, or "propensity to consume," is 0.9; over the year people are saving ten percent of their income.

Investment expenditure, on the other hand, is generally supposed to be more volatile. When businessmen are optimistic, they invest more than when they are pessimistic about the future. In addition, aggregate investment in any one year may be augmented by "Acts of God": hurricanes, floods, terrorist attacks— anything that destroys buildings, transport facilities, public utilities, or generally some parts of the country's infrastructure will require investment expenditure on repairs.

As for the expenditure by the government of, say, $80 billion, it can be regarded as being one part of a total expenditure on consumption of, say, $200 billion. Thus the $200 billion of aggregate consumption expenditure may be divided into $120 billion on *private* consumption goods and $80 billion on *public* consumption goods—the community being in effect constrained to buy these government-produced public goods by paying $80 billion to the government in the form of taxes.

Clearly if the government spends during the year another $2 billion on public goods, though without increasing taxation, aggregate consumption expenditure will increase to $102 billion; $82 billion on public consumption goods and $120 billion on private consumption goods.

It may be noted in passing, however, that a moderate rate of inflation—which has become virtually unavoidable in the West since World War II—operating within a progressive tax system transfers to the government more than an increase in tax that is proportional to the rate of inflation; in other words, a progressive tax system always transfers to the government some real increase of aggregate income even if the economy is not growing at all. Thus, unless governments continually reduce the tax structure (or people learn to improve their methods of avoiding tax) the public sector will grow over time.

3. If the reader can bear with some added complexity we can remove the tacit assumption of an autarkic economy, one that does not engage in foreign trade. It follows therefore that any import of goods amounts to a reduction of the domestic aggregate expenditure while, on the other hand, the export of goods becomes an addition to domestic aggregate expenditure. For if the country imports annually, say, $20 billion which, in the absence of imports would have been spent on domestically produced goods, then $20 billion less is left to spend on domestic goods. If, however, the country also exports goods worth $20 billion annually, such exports being domestically produced, the aggregate expenditure of the country is increased by $20 billion. This exact balance of payments in foreign trade is, however, not likely to exist in any one year. If then the value of the goods exported *exceeds* the value of the goods and materials imported by, say $4 billion, aggregate domestic expenditure in the year this occurs will have increased by this $4 billion.

In the determination of a country's national income and employment it is the aggregate expenditure on its domestic goods that matter. And this aggregate domestic expenditure is made up, or can be divided into, four components: consumption of domestically produced goods, business investment in domestic goods, expenditure by the government on domestically produced goods, and the country's expenditure on goods for export. The reader is not likely to be surprised to learn that a change in any of these four components might also generate changes in any or each of the other four.

4. A difference between short-term and long-term employment and a distinction between employment-creation and employment-diversion with respect to the economy as a whole has now to be considered. Both can be illustrated by a proposal to build some major project, say a new international airport.

Let us suppose that the building of the international airport will take three years and cost $12 billion, or $4 billion each year. The question that has to be answered is whether this $12 billion is a net increase in aggregate investment over the three years, for it is quite possible that raising the $4 billion each year for the building of the airport can only be done by "crowding out" of about $4 billion of other investments. If so, the employment generated each year by building the airport does not create employment in the economy at large. It merely diverts it from the employment that would else have taken place had the other $4 billion of investment not been "crowded out." Clearly if less than

$4 billion of investment had been "crowded out," there would be some addition to aggregate employment during the three years required to build the airport.

The employment, if any, so created may be termed short-term. Once completed, the number (if any) employed building the airport will be able to find work elsewhere only if, again, there is some increase in aggregate expenditure. Once built, however, there will also be employment opportunities in order to staff the many facilities provided in and about the airport precincts. This employment may be termed long-term—though not because those so employed will continue there for a long time, but only because employment will be *available* there for a long time: if some worker leaves, there will be a vacancy to be filled.

The question then arises: is this long-term employment of those working within and about the new airport a genuine creation of employment; a rise that is, in effect, an increase in the level of employment in the economy as a whole? Or is it, instead, only a diversion of employment from one part of the country to another, or from one sort of employment to the other? The answer, it transpires, is quite simple. Unless the aggregate expenditure of the economy increases, there is only employment-*diversion:* no additional employment is created in the economy at large. Although the possibility cannot be ruled out, there can be no reasonable expectation that people will spend a greater proportion of their income simply because a new airport has become available. People may indeed want to spend more on flying about the world now that an additional airport is there to serve them. But it certainly does not follow that thenceforth they will spend more of their income than hitherto. If they choose to spend more on flying, they will spend less on other goods and services—in effect a shift of demand from one good or service to another, so engendering a diversion of employment, not a creation of it, and therefore not increasing the level of employment in the economy at large.

What is said above applies equally to the building of passenger airliners and the additional personnel required to service them.[2]

5. So far we have established the fact that, within the country as a whole, only an increase in the aggregate expenditure on domestically produced goods can increase the level of income and employment. The reader may, however, have been left with the impression that an increase of, say, $2 billion per annum in aggregate domestic expenditure will result in an annual increase of income in

---

[2]The claim that the building of additional gambling casinos would be a means of "regenerating" the economy of a town or city is difficult to vindicate, not only in consideration of the above arguments, but also because the degree of such "regeneration," apart from infelicitous consequences, is certainly overestimated. The large sums people may spend in such casinos do nothing to increase aggregate expenditure in the economy and therefore do not create any additional employment there. What is spent in gambling amounts only to a transfer of such sums from losers to winners, some allowance being made for a small percentage of such monies that are necessary to pay the personnel and yield profits to the owners.

the economy of $2 billion and a corresponding increase in employment. We have now to show that this is not necessarily the case, even though it were the case that the weekly earnings of newly employed workers were the same irrespective of the industries affected or their location. Nor would it be true if, in addition, the amount of capital per worker used in any industry, or economic activity, affected by the increase in aggregate expenditure were the same.

For simplicity of exposition then, assuming that weekly earnings of all employees affected were equal and, also, that the capital-labor ratio were also equal, we shall broach the issue by restricting ourselves respectively to two limiting, or boundary, "macroeconomic" conditions: that of "full employment" and that of "low employment," beginning with the former.

Economists are reluctant to talk of "full employment" since it evokes a picture of the economy in which every worker in the country is satisfactorily employed —which has never been the case. We have to content ourselves with talking of "high employment" while recognizing that the proportion of the workforce employed is difficult to calculate. For, in addition to much changing of employment over a given period, there will be changes in sick leave, in vacations, in part-time or overtime work, etc., so that doubts may be cast on the reliability of the best estimates. The high level of employment we are constrained to talk about, however, is high enough to pose a risk of more than a moderate rate of inflation.

If, therefore, in circumstances in which the total productive capacity can no longer be expanded, the aggregate domestic expenditure increased by, say, $10 billion, although this would lead initially to a shortage of goods, it could eventually produce an equilibrium in the economy. In such an equilibrium, the value of the *unchanged* aggregate output of goods in the economy is increased by $10 billion so as to equal the initial $10 billion addition to the aggregate domestic expenditure. Thus, although there would then be roughly a proportional increase in all prices (and wages), the real position remains unchanged.

This resulting proportional rise in prices is, however, unlikely to be the end of the matter if, as is usually the case, people continue to seek to buy more goods than the economy can produce, so further raising prices and wages. An inflation so initiated can therefore come to an end only when, at the price level reached, the value of aggregate *domestic expenditure* no longer exceeds the value of aggregate *output,* given that the economy is producing at full capacity.[3]

It has therefore to be concluded that in this limiting case, an increase in aggregate domestic expenditure raises income—and may raise it far above the initial increase in aggregate domestic expenditure, although it does not, indeed cannot, increase "real" income and employment.

---

[3]It is generally supposed that the monetary authority, by curbing the growth of the money supply, can help to bring the inflation to a close. The freedom with which the monetary authority can act is, however, limited—as explained in Fallacy 12.

6. The case is quite different where there is an increase in aggregate expenditure during an economic depression, such as that which existed in Britain and America during the early 1930s. In such circumstances, the famous British economist, John Maynard Keynes, could legitimately assume that wages would continue to remain the same even though there were a significant increase in employment. An increase, for example, in aggregate domestic expenditure—whether by consumers, by investors, by the government (say, by reducing taxes, so increasing disposable income), or by exporters—will no longer generate inflation. Instead it will generate an increase in real income and employment, always assuming that there remains excess capacity of capital and labor in the economy.

In order, however, for the increase in income and employment to remain finite, so avoiding inflation, it is necessary that not all of any increase in income is spent. Suppose that, on average, only 80 percent of a primary increase in income is spent, or as the jargon has it, "the propensity to consume" is equal to 0.8. With this propensity to consume of 0.8, an initial increase of $2 billion in aggregate domestic expenditure does indeed create a primary increase in incomes equal to $2 billion. But those who receive this increase in income, involving, as it will, an increase in employment, do not spend it all—only 80 percent of it, the remaining 20 percent being saved. Since they spend 80 percent of $2 billion, or $1.6 billion, there is a further increase of incomes created equal to $1.6 billion. The recipients of this additional income of $1.6 million will then spend 80 percent of it, so generating a further increase of income equal to $1.28 billion, and so on. In time, therefore, this primary increase of income of $2 billion creates a secondary stream of income, the *total* increase of income (and consequent increase in employment) converging to equal $10 billion.[4]

The above exercise has, however, to be qualified to make allowance for other factors which act to reduce the net propensity to consume domestic goods. First, we have to recognize that the propensity to consume applies only to *disposable* income, that is income after tax has been deducted. Moreover, since some fraction of one's disposable income is also spent on imports, the proportion of any increase in income that is spent on domestically produced goods is further reduced. Once account is taken of such subtractions from any given increase in income, the net propensity to consume domestically produced goods may be reduced to two-thirds or even one-half, in which case the additional $2 billion of domestic expenditure results in a total increase of real income respectively of $6 billion or $4 billion.

---

[4]Readers having some acquaintance with mathematics will know (or can work out) that the series $1 + 4/5 + (4/5)^2 + (4/5)^3 + \dots (4/5)^n$, where n converges to ∞, is virtually equal to 5.

Fallacy 9

A Competitive Private Enterprise Economy Tends to Produce Economic Efficiency

1. It should first be acknowledged that liberal economists also regard a competitive private enterprise economy not only as one that tends to efficiency in production, but also as one that creates a bulwark for individual liberty. As has been repeatedly argued by such libertarian economists as the late Laureate, Milton Friedman, the preservation of freedom requires the elimination of the concentration of power in any agent or institution, including those of governments, and the distribution and social control of whatever power cannot be eliminated. This aspect of a free market economy can bear repeated emphasis.

We should, however, recognize that the free enterprise market economy today encompasses, at least in the countries of the West, only a proportion, and not always the larger proportion, of the total economy of these countries —the remainder (excluding the so-called black economy)—being the public economy in which products and services are provided by central and local governments. In Britain, the market economy comprises about a half of the total economy, and that proportion is more likely than not to dwindle over time as the Welfare State (including the spread of NGOs—Non-Governmental Organizations that provide or funnel state aid in one manner or another) continues to grow.

2. Turning to the belief of the greater economic efficiency of the competitive market economy, however, there are three aspects of economic efficiency to be

considered. The first is that most emphasized by liberal economists, efficiency in meeting people's wants: within the competitive market sector each person is free to choose the goods he wants and also to choose the amounts of each good at the market price. This aspect of efficiency may be conceded, although with some reservations about the economic justification of the set of prices set by the market—a provision the reader will understand better once we have discussed the third aspect of efficiency.

The second aspect of economic efficiency is that of producing the goods being consumed, or the services being used, at their lowest cost. Here, the competitive market can again be said to be more efficient than the public sector.

At the beginning of the Industrial Revolution in Britain, about the second half of the eighteenth century, the overwhelming proportion of the economy was operated by private enterprise. Those who read Adam Smith's *Wealth of Nations* (published in 1776) must have been convinced of this aspect of efficiency by, among other things, his simple examples of the production of basic goods in a competitive market economy. Certainly firms large and small had every incentive to seek ways of reducing the costs of their goods. One way was through the division of labor as Smith illustrated by describing the method being used in the production of pins; that of arranging for groups of employees to specialize exclusively in each of a number of successive single operations in shaping the pins.

It may be allowed that the private enterprise sector of the economy continues today to seek ways of reducing the cost of production of its goods, even though it is also characterized by a growing incentive to create ever more elaborate consumer innovations.

The third aspect of economic efficiency is the success achieved in the allocation of the resources of the economy so as to produce the combination of goods that would have the highest value for the community. It is in this aspect, however, that the competitive market fails.

Before discussing the reasons why the market fails to produce the ideal or "optimal" allocation of resources, let us define such optimality as one that results in the production of each of the different goods in such amounts that it is no longer possible—by changing the amounts of the goods produced— to make everyone in the community better off; put otherwise, optimality entails that it is not possible to make any one person better off without making one or more persons worse off, "a culmination devoutly to be wished." The further we are from this optimum position, the greater the "market failure."

This optimum position, or optimal allocation of resources, is not, of course, to be conceived as static, as a prevailing situation, but as a position that continually changes in response to any change in the conditions of demand and/or supply—in consequence of which the prices of some goods are apt to change as also are the prices of resources—of the different sorts of labor, land, and capital. What really concerns us, then, is whether, following such change, the competitive market economy has a *tendency* to move toward the corresponding optimal position.

3. Returning now to the prevalence of market failure, the chief causes in ascending order of importance are (1) the persistence of a number of monopolies (which, however, are by definition to be excluded from a competitive market economy), (2) the existence of unpriced but scarce natural (environmental) resources, (3) government intervention that alters prices through taxation, frequently by excise taxes or subsidies, and (4) the existence of what economists call "externalities" or are referred to also as "spillovers"—those incidental and presumably unintentional effects on the welfare of others, or on the welfare of society at large, generated in the production of certain goods, or generated by the consumption or use of such goods.

This last cause, the existence of spillovers, being the most important cause of market failure, is what we shall focus on from now on.

4. Prior to exhibiting how the incidence of spillovers acts to deflect the tendency of the economy to move toward an optimal allocation of resources, we have first to explicate the rationale of the necessary conditions for ascertaining its existence. These necessary conditions can be more easily understood if we assume, provisionally, that market failure is entirely *absent* in our private enterprise competitive economy which, therefore, will indeed tend to optimality.

Since the necessary conditions are expressed in terms of *marginal* costs and *marginal* valuations, their import in this connection requires that we understand the meaning of marginal as distinct from *average*. This is best done by a simple illustration.

The average cost of the production of a good is clearly obtained by dividing the total cost of its production by the number of goods produced. If, therefore, of a particular good only three units are produced, the first costing $8, the second costing $14, and adding a third unit an additional $20, the average cost of the three units is equal to $14. In contrast, since the marginal cost of production refers to the additional cost of production that is incurred in producing one additional good, the marginal cost of the first unit of good produced is, of course, $8. Producing an additional good costs an additional $14, which is therefore the marginal cost of producing two goods. And producing yet one more good will cost $20, this being the marginal cost of producing three goods, and so on.[1]

Similarly, when we turn from costs to valuations of goods—bearing in mind that, in economics, the valuation or worth of a thing to a person is the most he is willing to pay for it. If, in our simple example, of but three units of the good being produced, our chosen person will pay no more than $36 for the single available unit of this good, its marginal cost is $36. If, having already paid $36 for this good, another such good becomes available for which the most he will pay is $26, then the marginal valuation of buying two goods is $26. If again, after paying the $26 for a second good, he will pay no more than $22 for a third, his marginal valuation of buying three goods is this $22.

It follows from a comparison of the marginal valuations and the marginal costs of these three goods produced there is a net gain which is maximized by producing only three goods: producing a fourth good would only serve to reduce this gain. Let us make this quite explicit.

Should only one good be produced, there will be an excess gain equal to $28—the amount by which its marginal valuation of $36 exceeds its marginal cost of production of $8. The excess gain to be made by producing a second good is equal to $12, which is the amount by which the marginal valuation of

---

[1]Some readers may be puzzled by my illustration of a marginal (and average) cost that is increasing when more of the good is produced. He may think it more likely that marginal (and average) cost should fall as more is produced.

But in our assumed competitive economy in which each firm in an industry producing, say, only one good X, and producing it at its lowest average cost, we have also to bear in mind that the cost of a unit of X is equal to the expenditure on the combination of productive factors that are needed to produce that unit of X. And since in general the market prices of these productive factors (basically land, labor, and capital) will themselves alter whenever different amounts of goods in the economy are produced, the expenditure on them per unit of X (and on each unit of any other good) will also alter.

The simplest example possible would be an economy in which there are only two factors, labor and capital, a unit of good X using a *larger* proportion of labor than is used in a unit of the only other good Y. Given that the factor-endowment is fixed in that economy, a shift of aggregate expenditure on good X at the expense of good Y cannot of itself change the given amounts of labor and capital available in the economy: it can only change their prices.

Thus, if more of good X is to be produced, more of labor would be required than becomes available from producing less of good Y. Since, however, the amount of labor is fixed in supply, the increased demand for labor has the effect only of raising its market price, the reverse being true for the market price of capital.

But at these new market prices for labor and capital, the cost of good X will rise relative to the cost of good Y since good X uses proportionally more of the now-higher priced factor, labor, than does the other good Y.

Finally, since labor is now more expensive, the firms producing each good will economize by substituting more of the now-cheaper capital for labor, so enabling more of good X to be produced.

two goods (equal to $26) exceeds the marginal cost of production of the two goods (equal to $14). Finally, the excess gain from producing a third good is equal to $22 less $20, or only $2.

This net gain of $42 from producing only three goods is the most that can be derived. For if an additional good, a fourth good, is produced, it will be valued at less than $22, say $18, whereas the additional cost of producing will be more than $20, say $24. Hence, producing a fourth good would entail a loss of $6. It may be appropriate, then, to refer to this production of three goods, which yields the maximum net gain, as its "optimal output."

Now let us set a market price of $20 for this good. Then a person who is allowed to buy as many of these goods as he wants at this $20 price will choose to buy three of them, thereby maximizing his gain, this being equal to $24 ($16+$6+$2). Were he to buy a fourth good at $20, he would be worse off by $2 since, as stated above, he values it at no more than $18.

As for the person producing the good which sells at $20, he will gain most, $18 ($12+$6+$0), by choosing to produce only three of them, at which his marginal cost of producing three goods is equal to the $20 price of the good.

Clearly, this setting of the price of the good at $20 enables us to split this overall maximum gain of $42 from producing three goods into a gain of $24 for the consumer and a gain of $18 for the producer. What emerges from this setting of a $20 price in our simple example is that the optimal output of a good can now be defined as that output for which its competitive market price is equal to (or sometimes a bit greater than) its corresponding marginal cost, an expression that can therefore be regarded as the necessary condition for an optimal output of any good.

5. Applying this necessary condition for optimality to all the goods produced in the competitive market, where quite a number of competing firms are assumed to be producing each good and where, in general, a very large number of consumers of each good may be assumed, we shall find it expedient to express the necessary condition for optimality as requiring that the price of each good be *equal* to its corresponding marginal cost.[2]

We may take it for granted that in a competitive market economy the price of each good will tend to settle at the level at which the quantity of the good demanded by consumers is equal to the quantity produced. For if more of the

---

[2]To be sure, there can be instances in which a firm will maximize its profit by producing an output at which its marginal cost falls a bit short of the price of the good (since the production of an additional good would incur a marginal cost that is greater than its price). But there is nothing to be gained by being so fastidious as to express the condition in a more cumbersome form simply to ensure that we include such rare cases.

In any case, economists habitually assume continuity in their constructs since it simplifies the geometry or mathematics to which they frequently have recourse in demonstrating their theorems.

good were produced than were being purchased at the price, that price would start to fall, and vice versa.

Accepting the mainstream assumption that the marginal costs of production of an industry (eventually) rise as more of a good is produced, each of, say, 20 equally efficient firms[3] producing the same good will maximize its "profits" by producing an output at which its marginal cost is equal to the prevailing market price.

As for the consumers of any good, although the amounts purchased at the market price will, in general, differ from one consumer to another, each one of them maximizes his gain by purchasing that amount of the good which equates his marginal valuation to the market price of the good.

We may therefore conclude by affirming that only when the necessary conditions are met in the production of all goods will the resultant outputs all be optimal.[4]

6. We must now remove our provisional assumption, introduced in Section 4, of no market failure whatsoever, which implies not only that neither monopolies or unpriced natural resources exist, but also that no spillovers are generated in the production of any good. If, however, say damaging spillovers are indeed generated in the production of any good, the real or "social" cost will exceed the firms' private costs. The optimal amount of each good produced has therefore now to be more comprehensively defined as the amount at which its social marginal cost of production is equal to the competitive market price—this social marginal cost being calculated simply by adding to the firms' private costs of each unit of the good produced, the cost also of the spillover damages it generates.

Economic activities in the modern economy generate a variety of familiar spillovers, some local, some reaching beyond the boundaries of the nation state. They include noise, stench, air and water pollution, overcrowding, ugly

---

[3]No problem arises if firms are not equally efficient. A less efficient firm will have a higher marginal cost for any output as a result of which it will produce a smaller output and earn a smaller "profit."

[4]It is sometimes argued that an optimal allocation of resources requires no more than prices be *proportional* to their corresponding marginal costs; hence, if the price of each good were, say, 20 percent above its corresponding marginal cost, an optimal position of the market economy is secured.

Valid though this is, such an equilibrium would be stable only in an imperfectly competitive market economy. In a perfectly competitive market economy it would be unstable since the manager of each firm would perceive that he could further increase his "profit" by expanding output until, indeed, the marginal cost did in fact equal the corresponding market price of the good. But when there are no more resources available in the market economy the attempt to expand can only lead to a rise in the price of the resources needed as firms seek to expand. Thus the situation becomes stable only when, in the production of all goods, the resulting marginal costs of each good is again equal to its corresponding market price.

buildings, toxic wastes, the destruction of animal and plant species, and the damage to our health by the proliferation of chemical products, such as drugs, cosmetics, and sprays.

Once we become aware of a spillover, we can deal with it in a number of ways, sometimes in an economic combination of a variety of different ways. Apart from wholly banning the product of a good, or methods of bureaucratic control of its production, which are seldom favored by economists, the more familiar ways include the relocation of the offending plant or works, the employment of technological devices to reduce or eliminate the extent of the pollution generated, or the imposition of an excise tax calculated to be equal to the cost of the *marginal* (residual) spillover. This latter, popular among economists, is often referred to as a pollution tax or an effluent tax. And where, as is often the case, the spillover cost per unit output remains constant, this tax is equal to this per unit spillover cost since when imposed it reduces the output to that at which the social marginal cost is indeed equal to the price of the good.

A simple example will illustrate. Consider a dye works situated on the banks of a river into which it pours its waste products so destroying the fish in the vicinity and otherwise spoiling the recreation once enjoyed by families living near the downstream river banks. The damage inflicted being calculated at $16 for every gallon of dye produced, the effluent tax is set at $16 per gallon produced by the works. Adding this tax to the production cost of, say, $20 per gallon, the social cost per gallon that now has to be borne by the dye works, comes to $36. Consequently the effluent tax results in the dye works producing the optimal amount of the dye—that at which the marginal social cost is equal to the market price.

Two caveats, before ending this section. First, it is often difficult to measure the cost of the spillover generated by the production of successive goods. In such cases a "guesstimate" of the cost, when applied, results in an approximation to the optimal output of the good, which is better than taking no action at all. In other words, there is a presumption that if some amount of the spillover is reduced then, even if that amount is too little or too much, the community will be better off than it would be if all the spillover generated remains uncorrected.

Second, it has to be recognized that since there will also be costs incurred in any endeavor to realize an optimal output for a spillover-generating good, whether by taxation, relocation, or by any other method, and possibly also an expansion of bureaucracy, it may be more economic to refrain from taking action when for the output being produced the divergence between the social marginal cost and the market price is not very great.

7. And there we might rest our case were it not for a stir created by, and credence given to a theorem, or rather a conclusion reached, in a journal article in 1960, which purported to show that in a competitive economy having

well-defined property rights in all scarce resources, private enterprise alone would suffice to realize optimal outputs—no state intervention being necessary.

Were such a theorem valid, all the preceding exposition would amount to "Love's Labour Lost." Not surprisingly, the theorem became popular among businesspeople, also at the time (sad to admit) among some economists, particularly "free-market" economists. Since the theorem is still occasionally quoted in defense of unfettered enterprise, we shall use up a little more space in dissecting it.

The homely example introduced in this article, though one from which—notwithstanding that it was followed by a leisurely exposition of other examples—this startling conclusion is drawn, is that of a rancher's cattle, a number of which cattle stray through a gap in the fence, thereby damaging the crops in the adjacent farmland.

With such an example it is not difficult to show that whether the property rights to the farmland belong to the farmer, in consequence of which the rancher has to pay the farmer for the losses incurred by his straying cattle, or whether, instead, the farmland is the property of the rancher, in which case he will exact payment from the farmer for preventing such losses, the outcome is uniquely determined. This is because the loss suffered by the farmer is uniquely determined, being equal to the market value of the amount of his crops he loses.

8. This neat solution which endeared itself to the business community cannot, however, be generalized to all spillovers: in fact, it is a very special case.

First, the unique optimal solution arises from a unique cost of the spillovers in this case being calculated by reference to the market price of the crops that are lost to the farmer. Should the spillover generated by one or more firms be one that takes the form instead of a pollutant that damages the health or welfare of individuals, the cost of the pollutant generated by any unit of the good *cannot* be costed simply by reference to a *market* price for a reduction in health or welfare. The pollutant is in fact subjectively valued; by reference, that is, to the compensation required either by the victims of the pollutant or else required by the firm generating the pollution to induce him to reduce it. In this far more usual case, it will indeed matter whether the business has a right to pollute the atmosphere or whether, instead, the victims have a legal right to a pollution-free atmosphere—this atmosphere, in effect, being the scarce resource to which the property rights have to be assigned.

Since economists are aware that, in general, the smallest sum a person is willing to accept to induce him to forgo a good (or to bear with a "bad") is *greater* (sometimes very much greater) than the most he is willing to pay, or can afford to pay, to acquire a good (or to avoid a "bad"), there will be two different evaluations of a unit of any pollutant, entailing two different *social* marginal costs and, therefore, two different optimal outputs of any good, according to which of the two parties owns the relevant property rights.[5]

It follows that if the people who will suffer from the pollution generated by one or more firms have property rights in the ambient atmosphere, the resulting social marginal cost will generally be higher than if, instead, the property rights in the ambient atmosphere belong to the firms generating the pollution. In consequence, the optimal output of the good in question will be smaller in the former case than in the latter.

9. Yet more important is that although extending property rights to arable land or mineral land, possibly to small lakes or stretches of a river, may work well enough, in other cases, certainly in all the substantial cases, the granting of property rights is quite impracticable.

Property rights in forest lands do not work well—not unless lumber companies are restricted to areas sufficiently small that, over the long term, their profits depend upon both selective logging and reforestation. Unfortunately, nearly all tropical rain forests, although officially under government control, are treated as a commons. Such forests are being rapidly destroyed both by large companies using chain saws and tractors and also by migrant peasants using "slash-and-burn" methods to level countless acres of forest in order to clear more space for the planting of crops. Thus no account is taken of the destruction of species, of the cumulative effect on the earth's atmosphere and climate, or of the losses to be borne by future generations.

Deep sea fishing is another instance where, although property rights over areas of the ocean are conceivable, they would be virtually impossible to enforce.

---

[5]An extreme example will highlight this difference.

Mr. Jones inherits a site near Smallville on which he proposed to build a glue factory, one which will emit malodorous fumes. Since the operation of the factory will emit about the same amount of fumes no matter how much or how little glue is produced, the only feasible alternative is that of relocating the factory to a more desolate area.

If there is no law to prevent Mr. Jones building his factory near Smallville, the residents meet together and finally agree to offer Mr. Jones as much as $300,000, if necessary, not to site his factory near their town. But Mr. Jones will not accept less than $500,000 since this is the loss he will have to bear if he builds his factory in a more remote area. His decision to go ahead and site his factory in Smallville is, he will argue, the right economic decision. For were he indeed to build it elsewhere, as suggested, his loss of $500,000 would exceed the gain of $300,000—so making the community as a whole, himself included, worse off.

However, suppose an appeal by the mayor of Smallville is successful, the ruling of the Courts being that Mr. Jones will have to compensate the residents of Smallville if he builds his factory there. But the minimal sum that the residents are prepared to accept as compensation for bearing with the fumes of Mr. Jones's factory is $840,000, which obliges him to relocate it elsewhere. The mayor may well argue that this is the right economic decision since, if the factory were built near Smallville, a net loss to the community (including Mr. Jones) would be involved—the saving of $500,000 to Jones being smaller than the loss of $840,000, the cost of the factory's spillover that has to be borne by the residents.

Legislation devised to preserve the fish population by rationing the catch of fish, or some sorts of fish, are wasteful, difficult to monitor, and unpopular in the industry.

In other cases, the conferring of property rights is a nonstarter. There is no way in which the earth's atmosphere can be parcelled out to corporations or individuals to enable them to charge others for its use. As a result, the earth's atmosphere will continue to be used as a common sewer, at least in the absence of taxes or prohibitions on polluting emissions.[6]

We could continue, but enough has been said to conclude that an extension of clearly defined property rights for all scarce resources employed in a competitive economy will *not*, contrary to what is asserted in the article, tend to produce an optimal allocation of resources. The wide variety of spillover effects ensure that—save for specially contrived instances in which the activities of one firm results in a loss of the marketable output of another adjacent firm or firms—allocative efficiency will not be realized no matter how competitive the economy.

10. A final consideration may be invoked to reinforce the pessimism of the above conclusion.

The sheer rapidity of technological advances over the past half century has unavoidably extended the time lag between the emergence of a new spillover and our awareness of its prevalence and potency. Moreover, in many instances the damage caused by the spillover eludes economic calculation and therefore any hope of realizing an optimal allocation of resources.

Countless new chemical substances are used each year in popular products that fill the shelves of our supermarkets: in women's cosmetics, in hair dyes and hair sprays, in aerosols, in cleaning powders and cleaning fluids, also for adding color, flavor, or longevity to the foodstuffs we ingest. Our knowledge of the effect on our health of such new chemical substances, and of new drugs on display at the local pharmacy, emerge only slowly and possibly after much injury has been inflicted.

By the time it was discovered that Thalidomide, a drug prescribed by doctors for calming pregnant women, could also act to cause babies to be born with distorted or shrunken limbs, it was too late to prevent thousands of men and women from having their lives marred by shocking and frustrating deformities.

Again, by the time scientists discovered that the release of chlorofluorocarbon gases being released by the use of aerosols and refrigerants was active in eroding the earth's ozone mantle which serves to protect us from harmful radiation, much damage had already been done that, possibly, cannot be undone.

---

[6]Nor is anti-pollution legislation always effective. The installation, say, of tall chimney stacks can reduce the amount of smoke descending on the local population. But, as we now know, windborn gases formed by burning fossil fuels move across national boundaries, to fall in other countries as acid depositions.

A Subsidy to University Education Is Justified Since It Promotes Equality of Opportunity and Confers Benefits on Society as a Whole

1. The student population in Britain before World War II was about 50,000. Today it is about two million, of which two-thirds are in full-time education. Since annual grants in excess of £5 billion are paid to universities in order to enable them to maintain university fees far below their full costs (state subsidies to universities in the United States in 2002 amounted to $66 billion; federal subsidies added billions more), it is not unreasonable for taxpayers to wonder if they are getting their money's worth. Some taxpayers may console themselves with the thought that, even though they may be uncertain about the sort of benefits that a student's education is supposed to confer on others than himself, a subsidy that enables university fees to be set far below their costs does indeed promote equality of opportunity, opening the door of university education to students whose parents are too poor to pay the full costs.

In this chapter, however, I hope to convince the reader that both beliefs are economic fallacies: the belief that the subsidy is justified since university education confers benefits on society as a whole and, also, the belief that only a sizable subsidy will enable the children of poor parents to benefit from a university education.

It may as well be stated at the start that among economists there is a general presumption against subsidies. Unless there are economically justifiable grounds for the subsidy in question, it must result in "too much" of the subsidized good being produced.[1] Our task here is to reveal just how this simple theorem may be applied to the subsidy offered to universities, on the provisional assumption that the benefits of university education accrue wholly to commercially minded students.

2. Before preparing the ground for embarking on this task, a digression about the treatment of this subsidy is revealing. Currently, using Britain as the example, we may suppose that the government has decided to pay £30,000 to each student willing to take a standard three-year university course; this being the amount necessary to cover all his costs, both the full university fees and living, or maintenance, costs over the three-year period.

If now the government were persuaded to offer each of the two million young people who would have enrolled as students, the choice of using his grant of £30,000 in any way he wishes, we can be quite certain that each of a very large number of them would elect instead to use the money for uses other than a university education. Some might choose to invest all or some of the money in investments yielding an annual income, others might use a proportion of it on travel, on visceral pleasures, or on "wine, women, and song."

No matter how each of them uses this money it does not, however, cost the government, or rather the taxpayer, any more than if each of the two million had received the £30,000 conditional upon his becoming a university student. In contrast, many—almost certainly the majority of the two million—would indeed be better off when they are allowed to use the £30,000 in any way they pleased.

Since taxpayers are no worse off when the two million young people are allowed to spend the money as they please, while these young people are indeed better off when left free to choose how to spend the £30,000, the community as a whole may be said to be better off—with the student population resulting now being far below two million.

3. Although the above exercise should suffice to sow doubts in the reader's mind of the economic wisdom of offering subsidies to university students, either directly or via student fees that are well below costs, we shall now knuckle down to the task of revealing that, allowing initially that students are "economic beings"—that is, commercially minded—the student subsidy produces too large a student population. (Again, too large in the sense that there will be net economic gains in reducing the number to an "optimal size" that is soon to be explained.)

---

[1]The economists' conclusion that a subsidy of a good results in "too much" of it being produced follows from the familiar demonstration that the resultant fall in the unit cost of the good leads to the production of an output that is in excess of that produced by the market equilibrium in the absence of the subsidy. Reducing this subsidized output to the original market-equilibrium output can then be shown to increase economic efficiency—in the sense that it will increase aggregate income in the economy.

Our task will be made easier if, having conceived of the money spent on university education as an investment, we resort again to our pedagogical device of first addressing ourselves to extreme cases. The first case is that in which the student himself bears the full cost of his education including all his maintenance costs over the three-year period; the second case being that in which all such costs are borne by the taxpayer so that, so far as the student is concerned, his three years at the university are free.

We begin with the economic axiom that is of a piece with the demand for a good: the greater the amount of investment undertaken in the economy the lower is the annual rate of return on any additional investment. This axiom is commonly referred to by economists as that of diminishing marginal returns to investment.[2] Thus, if we take a unit of investment to measure, say, $2 million, the first unit of investment in any particular industry might yield an annual return equal to 16 percent per annum, an additional unit of investment yielding a return of 14 percent, a third of 13 percent, and so on.

There will, of course, be many different ways of investing money, from which we will select the existing investment in the *A* industry, yielding a marginal rate of return of 12 percent, and the existing investment in the *B* industry which yields no more at the margin than 8 percent. Such a situation, however, would not continue for long since the total investment in both *A* and *B* can be redistributed to economic advantage. It may not be easy, however, to transfer units of investment from *B* to *A,* where the yield is higher. Therefore, instead, any additional investment will be placed in *A* rather than in *B,* since investment in *A* yields 4 percent more than in *B.* As indicated, however, the return to additional units of investment in any one industry diminishes, from which we may infer that the higher yield in *A* will fall as investment in *A* increases until the *A* investment yields no more than in the *B* industry.

We conclude that for an optimal allocation of investment as between *A* and *B* the marginal rate of return will have to be the same in each: for any other allocation in which the rate of return to one form of investment were higher than in the other would entail an economic loss as compared with the optimal allocation, in which the same amount of *total* investment is allocated between the two investment opportunities as to produce equal rates of return.[3]

Generalizing from the above example, it may be inferred that the total investment in the economy is optimal when the marginal rate of return in each distinct

---

[2]This diminishing marginal return to investment should be plausible enough if we think of this investment as increasing the capacity of an industry to produce a good *X.* An additional amount of this investment will then yield a lower return than preceding units of investment if only because the additional amount of good *X,* which can be produced with the additional capacity, will be purchased only if the price of *X* itself is lowered.

[3]In fact, investments may be ranked according to risk, the greater the risk the higher the actuarial rate of return. We ignore this complication since including it would prolong the exposition without in any way affecting our conclusions.

form of investment is exactly the same. And since spending money on university education is one form of investment, an optimal investment requires that the marginal rate of return in university education also be equal to that on all other kinds of investment. Indeed, since the university offers many different courses, the equality in the marginal rate of return must be equal for *each* course offered.

4. Although the economist is able to compare and therefore to rank alternative "investment streams" over time in various ways, it will be convenient to compare them by reducing them to an internal rate of return (IRR), since the IRR may be regarded as corresponding to the yield, or rate of return, used in the above exposition. First, we must explain the terms "stream of investment" and the IRR.

By a stream of investment the economist has in mind a succession of annual net benefits over time that results from an initial cost during the first year, or several years, of an investment. If the entire cost of the investment occurs during the first year, which we might designate as y_0, the following years in which the net benefits accrue may be designated y_1, y_2, y_3, and so on until the final year, y_n.

A simple example would be −200, 110, 121. The *minus* 200 being the cost of the investment in the original year, y_0, whereas the 110 and 121 are the *net* benefits that accrue in the two following years—the life-span of the benefits of this investment being only two years.

The figures in the above example have been chosen to yield an IRR equal to 10 percent. For if the net benefit of 110 in y_1 and the net benefit of 121 in y_2 are discounted to the present, to year y_0, they will together amount to 200, just equal to initial cost of 200 in y_0.[4]

This simple example illustrates the definition of the IRR as that rate of discount which when applied to each of the net benefits reduces them to a present value, at y_0, exactly equal to the initial cost.

5. If we now suppose that the IRR for all investment in the economy were equal to 10 percent, then an optimal allocation of investment in the economy as a whole would require that the investment in university education should also be equal to 10 percent. Indeed, in an ideal perfectly competitive economy in which investment everywhere yielded an IRR equal to 10 percent, banks would also be lending at 10 percent.

It follows that if a poor student borrowed from the bank an amount necessary to finance his education, he would gain by so borrowing—in that (after repaying

---

[4]The formula in elementary textbooks appears as defining the IRR as that r for which $\Sigma_{i=1}^{n}[Bi/(l + r)^i] = K_0$, where B_i is the net benefit in the ith year, r equals the rate of interest (expressed as a fraction of one), and K_0 the cost of the investment in the original year y_0.

If the simple investment stream in the text were altered to read −200, 100, 100, the IRR would in fact be zero. Were the net benefits *less* than 100, 100, the IRR would be negative.

We might note that for cases in which the initial costs were spread over two or more years, or where subsequent net benefits were negative, the IRR would be more comprehensively defined as that r for which $\Sigma_{i=0}^{n}[Bi/(l + r)^i] = 0$.

the bank) his subsequent earnings would exceed those he could expect to make in the absence of his university education—so long as his net benefit arising from his university education would yield an IRR greater than 10 percent.[5] But once student numbers taking that particular university course increased to the point that the IRR on university education declined to 10 percent, there would be no further gain from taking that course; an optimal number of students in that course will have been reached.

It transpires that exactly the same calculation has to be made by the rich student who does not have to borrow from the bank, since he too will have to forgo the 10 percent IRR he could earn on all other investment opportunities if he elected instead to invest in a university education. Again, as with the poor student, the rich student will gain by investing in a university education only so long as the resulting IRR from so investing exceeds 10 percent. Once the number of students enrolling for the same course increases so that the resulting IRR from his university education declines to 10 percent, there will be no further inducement for students to enrol in the course: an optimal number of students for that course will have been reached.

6. Although by now I expect the penny will have dropped, we may be yet more explicit by invoking hypothetical magnitudes so as to compare the two extreme cases we posited earlier: (A), that in which the student himself (whether he borrows or not) pays the full cost of his three-year period at the university, and (B), that in which all the costs of his three-year attendance at the university is paid for by the taxpayer. The full costs for each of the three years spent in university education we assume to be equal to £10,000. After graduation, we suppose a period of 30 years before retirement, during which the earnings may be such that net benefits accrue annually to the student—net benefits being defined as the *excess* of his annual earnings above the earnings he could have expected in the absence of his university education.

Since in case (A) where we are to suppose that already an optimal number of students are in university education, the IRR from investing in such education will be no greater than 10 percent, equal also to the 10 percent IRR on all other investments. Thus, following his three years of university education, costing him £10,000 each year, his profile of net benefits, or net earnings, for the remaining 30 years before his retirement may take any form consistent with an IRR of 10 percent. Generally speaking, the actual stream of annual net earnings will begin low, rising thereafter, and possibly sinking a bit before retirement. Whatever the actual shape of the profile, however, we could reshape it to yield a constant annual net earnings provided such an investment stream will also result in an IRR of 10 percent. Adopting this equivalent profile, say it comes to £400 each

---

[5]No matter how and when he rearranges his repayment to the bank, makes no difference to our conclusion.

year for the 30 years, makes the (A) extreme case simpler to compare with the (B) extreme case.

The two alternative investment streams therefore appear as follows:

(A) $-10,000, -10,000, -10,000, 400, 400, 400 \ldots \ldots \ldots, 400.$

(the final 400 appearing thirty years after the first 400)

(B) $-10,000, -10,000, -10,000, 0, 0, 0, \ldots \ldots \ldots, 0.$

The zeros in the (B) case result from the large number of students continuing to enroll in university courses when they cost each student nothing (being wholly subsidized) until eventually there is no further gain in doing so, the net benefits having sunk to zero. In the (B) case, therefore, the IRR is necessarily negative—certainly not a good investment of the taxpayers' money. In these latter circumstances, however, the poor student would indeed be able to argue that it is just as well that university education be subsidized since, if he had to borrow, he could never be able to repay the amount he would need to borrow form the banks to cover the full costs of his university education.

7. We may conclude:

(1) That when regarding university education as an investment, an optimal number of students—overall, and also for each distinct course—is attained only when all students, rich or poor, are required to pay the full costs of their university education. Given this optimal number of students, the future net earnings of each graduate ensures an IRR equal to the 10 percent we have assumed to prevail in all other investments.

(2) More generally we may infer that the larger the subsidy to the student the greater will be the number of students in excess of the optimal student population and the lower, therefore, will be their annual net earnings.

Once we relax our provisional assumption of commercially minded students and allow that some young people want to enter a profession or vocation that also provides them with non-pecuniary advantages, such as the prestige associated with the profession or vocation, opportunities for moving in a higher social circle or for public recognition, and so on, it follows that such students are prepared to accept—in exchange for such "psychic" income—a somewhat lower level of annual net earnings than would otherwise be necessary. The optimal number of students training for this profession will then be larger than it would be if only monetary returns mattered.

As for benefits that may be conferred on the rest of society, so long as such benefits are tangible they do not warrant subsidies to students training for any profession that incidentally provide such benefits. These benefits, being positive, are to be dealt with as indicated in Fallacy 9; that is, by lowering the unit cost of the service by the value of the positive spillovers it generates, thereby expanding the supply of the spillover-generating service, until its *social* marginal cost (less than its private marginal cost) is equal to the market price of the service.

8. The obvious fact that the ideal world of perfect competition and with only one IRR in the economy, which we have assumed for expository purposes, differs from the actual economy, one in which investments are classified according to risk, and in which banks discriminate according to the credit worthiness and collateral of their customers, one in which a small proportion of students will fail to graduate, and so forth, does not of itself obviate the general conclusions we have reached. Although it cannot be gainsaid that in the actual economy it becomes more difficult at any time to determine the optimal student population, we can be sure that, whatever it is, it is more likely to be reached by a scheme in which students pay the full cost of their education than a scheme in which students receive a subsidy no matter how modest. We can be equally sure that the larger the student subsidy, the larger will be the excess over the optimal student population, and therefore also the lower will be the students' net earnings after graduating.

Finally, the reader is to be reminded of the *ceteris paribus* clause which, of course, applies to any economic analysis. He has therefore to bear in mind also that there are continual changes in aggregate income and in its distribution over time, the same applying to the prices of goods and to the rates of return on the different types of investment. Each and any of such changes are likely to affect the actual size of the optimal student population. For this reason the economist habitually expresses his conclusions in terms of tendencies. In respect of student numbers, he will therefore state that meeting the necessary conditions ensures a *tendency* to produce an optimal number of students—the necessary conditions, as indicated, being that students pay the full costs of their university education. And his more general conclusion will take the form of a statement that the larger the student subsidy, the greater the *tendency* for student numbers to exceed the optimal student population; and the lower will the student's subsequent net earnings *tend* to be.

9. There are other incidental but significant advantages from removing the student subsidy.

Once students are required to pay the full costs of their university courses, it may be anticipated with absolute confidence that there would be a drastic diminution in the enrollment of quasi-ideological courses, to say nothing of the variety of bizarre and fatuous or "Mickey Mouse" university courses that, over the past few decades, have proliferated with increasing abandon within the curricula of British and U.S. universities. There may be little if any demand for students graduating from such outlandish courses. Yet the opportunities for enjoyment and revelry provided by the social facilities for students in the modern university is apparently regarded as ample compensation for the meagre prospects that await them in the real world.

What is more, once students have to bear the full costs of their education not only will they tend to choose university courses that prepare them for well-paid vocations, they will also become increasingly reluctant to engage in the occasional orgy of campus destruction, to indulge in absurd self-injurious student "strikes," or in other disruptive activities.

THE NATIONAL DEBT IS A BURDEN ON FUTURE GENERATIONS

1. This vintage fallacy was in fact also propagated by the late President Eisenhower in May 1963, when he attacked the late President Kennedy's administration for engaging in deficit finance, thereby increasing the public debt. "In effect," he asserted, "we are stealing from our grandchildren in order to satisfy our desires of today" (*Daily Telegraph,* May 15, 1963). That idea has been picked up by many commentators since, especially in the United States. A fallacy of such distinguished provenance is worth dissecting, so we shall take our time in doing so.

2. The existing public debt is the amount that the government owes to all those people or institutions that, over the past, have lent to the government in exchange for issues of government bonds yielding a fixed rate of interest. Thus, if the United States government were next year to borrow $40 billion by issuing, say, five percent bonds to that amount, which will be bought by the public, it will increase the American national debt by $40 billion. Since the government will then have to pay out in each subsequent year to these new bond-holders five percent on their holdings of $40 billion of bonds, the addition to the government's annual expenditure is equal to $2 billion, at least as a maximum (as we shall see).

Provisionally, we shall suppose that this new issue of $40 billion of five percent government bonds is bought up entirely by nationals—by residents in the United States. Now, if the government were to use this $40 billion borrowed from the public "wastefully," that is to say, to spend it on goods and services produced during that year (in preference to raising the $40 billion to pay for these goods and services wholly by taxation) then, indeed, it would have to increase taxation each year by $2 billion in order to meet the $2 billion interest payments.[1]

But can this additional annual tax of $2 billion be properly regarded as a burden on the nation as a whole? True, taxpayers do indeed have to pay an additional annual tax of $2 billion from their incomes. And to that extent they are worse off. But then, the bond-holders are to receive each year an addition to their incomes of $2 billion. The nation as a whole, therefore, is neither worse nor better off. What takes place is, in effect, no more than a *transfer* of income from taxpayers to bond-holders.

It may be easier to recognize the import of such a transfer if we imagine that the total number of income earners in this nation were exactly ten million, and each of them had bought exactly $2,000 worth of bonds. Each taxpayer would therefore have to contribute an additional $100 in tax but would also receive each year $100 as interest on his $2,000 of bonds: income-wise being therefore no worse off or better off than he was prior to the increase in the national debt. The fact that not all the taxpayers buy the same amount of the issue of government bonds does not, of itself, alter the conclusion that the nation as a whole is no worse off when there is an effective transfer of income from some members of the nation to other members.

3. But the case in which the government is so improvident as to spend the whole of the $40 billion it has raised from its new bond issue is obviously an extreme case. It is more likely to spend at least some of the $40 billion so raised on acquiring assets that yield an annual return. In the limiting case in which the government uses the $40 billion to invest solely in projects that yield a return of just five percent, there would be no need whatever for additional taxation to "service" the government bonds issued. Bond-holders would, of course, continue to receive between them their annual $2 billion of interest on their bonds, only now this interest is paid directly from the government's earning of $2 billion annual return on its investment of the $40 billion—no additional taxation being necessary.

What is more, a prudent government may be able to invest in projects that will, on average, yield more than five percent, which will enable it to reduce tax rates or else increase its annual expenditure, so increasing the gain to the nation.

4. In order to impress the reader with the validity of the preceding argument, let us elaborate a little.

---

[1]Although far less likely, the government—instead of raising taxes by $2 billion in order to pay the annual interest payments on the $40 billion—could reduce its annual public expenditure by $2 billion, in which case the "burden" may be regarded as the loss of $2 billion each year of public goods and services. This does not affect the analysis, however, since this loss each year of $2 billion is offset each year by the interest of $2 billion collected by the bond-holders.

First, there is no justification in regarding the purchase by nationals of the $40 billion of government bonds as itself a burden since anyone who chooses to purchase these government bonds does so of his own free will rather than using the money instead to invest or to consume goods during that year. And the fact that he chooses to invest his money that year in government bonds in anticipation of an annual increase in his income over future years can in no way bring his annual increase of income into question. Thus, the resulting additional annual income to bond-holders of $2 billion would indeed imply that the economy as a whole has a higher income than it would otherwise enjoy—except in the particular case mentioned, in which the government, having spent the $40 billion received from its bond sales, uses the sum entirely to finance its current public expenditure that year. In that particular case, as shown, taxpayers as a whole will be less well off inasmuch as they will have to pay an additional $2 billion in taxes. Yet in that rare and limiting case, the pluses and minuses cancel out, in consequence of which for the economy as a whole there is no net loss (or gain) of income arising from increasing the national debt by $40 billion.

Secondly, insofar as the government does not use the $40 billion wastefully or entirely wastefully, there will be some net increase in the income of the economy. To be sure, the net increase in the income of the economy might yet be appreciably larger if the government invests the whole of the $40 billion in profitable investment—or if, instead, those who purchased the bonds chose themselves to invest $40 billion in high-yielding assets.

5. There is, however, a later twist given to the burden argument which is of auxiliary interest. This new burden argument is developed from the worst-case scenario already mentioned, and then builds on the assumption that the nation's annual rate of investment—taken to be equal to its annual rate of saving—diminishes over time as the total stock of its capital (its industrial stock of plant and machinery, etc.) grows; the greater the existing stock of capital, the lower is the annual rate of investment and, therefore, the smaller will be the accumulated stock of capital at any future date.

Now if the total of the national debt were equal, say, to $200 billion, and all of that money had been used wastefully, the owners of the $200 billion of government bonds are apt to believe that they have actually accumulated $200 billion of real assets. In consequence they will annually save less than they otherwise would and, therefore, the accumulated stock of capital at some future date —say, two generations hence, will not be so great as it might otherwise have been. It should be noted, however, that this negative relation between the accumulated stock of capital and the rate of investment assumed in the preceding paragraph can be entirely disregarded without making any difference to our conclusion. For in so far as the government "wastefully" uses any part of the sums raised by increasing the national debt, the rate of current investment is also necessarily reduced, since instead of using their savings in buying government bonds people would have put their money into private investment yielding a *real* annual return. Hence, the more "wasteful" is the government when increasing the national debt, the smaller will be the rate of current investment and, therefore, the slower will be the growth of its accumulated capital stock—notwithstanding which, as indicated, the conclusion remains that the material standards enjoyed by future generations will certainly exceed those enjoyed by us today.

Needless to say, there is no need, indeed no warrant, for invoking the emotive term "burden" in this or any other economic analysis.

6. So far we have followed custom in assuming that the United States government bonds issued in any year are bought up entirely by U.S. residents. Although this may be true—and "burden-mongers" have based their argument on this assumption—it is likely that some of these bonds are purchased by foreigners. It is of ancillary interest therefore to enquire whether it makes any difference to our conclusions if, indeed, U.S. government bonds are bought by foreigners. The short answer is yes.

The difference to our conclusions can be more starkly exhibited if we make the extreme assumption that all of a $40 billion issue of the U.S. government bonds in a particular year are bought up entirely by residents in Britain. If now the U.S. government uses this $40 billion "wastefully"—using the $40 billion received from British residents solely to meet its current public expenditures in that year—then in all subsequent years it will have to pay these British bondholders $2 billion, which it can raise simply by adding $2 billion to its annual tax bill. Since no U.S. resident purchased any of this $40 billion bond issue, the interest of $2 billion is collected wholly by British; nothing by U.S. residents. Since, as distinct from the case where the $40 billion bond issue is taken entirely by U.S. residents, there is now no offsetting gain of $2 billion per annum in the United States. There will therefore be an annual net loss to the United States of this $2 billion (incidentally, the conclusion will be the same if, instead, the U.S. government used the $40 billion subscribed by British residents solely to reduce taxation during that year).

If, on the other hand, the government used this $40 billion only for investment in projects that yielded at least an annual return of five percent, it would have at its disposal in all subsequent years at least an additional $2 billion. Consequently, no additional taxes whatever need be levied, and therefore no "burden" has to be borne. And should the projects yield more than five percent, a reduction in taxation would be possible.

From these two limiting cases in which only British residents subscribe to the $40 billion bond issue, the more of the $40 billion used by the U.S. government in profitable investment the smaller will be the tax burden—becoming zero, or possibly a net gain, should the entire $40 billion be profitably invested.

7. Let us summarize:

(1) Restricting ourselves first to the supposed case that only U.S. residents hold all U.S. national debt, then,

(a) Even in the very worst case scenario in which, over all past years during which the national debt has accumulated, the government did not use any portion at all to invest in a profitable project, there is no tax burden whatever: simply a transfer from taxpayers as a whole to bond-holders as a whole.

(b) What is more, whether or not we accept the assumption that as the nation's stock of capital grows over time its annual rate of investment declines, whenever the government uses a part of the sums raised by increasing the national debt wastefully the resultant rate of the accumulation of the stock of capital becomes less than it otherwise would be. However, since the material wealth of future generations will certainly exceed that of the present generation, even if there is no increase whatsoever in the nation's stock of capital, one is compelled to reject as pure fantasy the late President Eisenhower's declaration (echoed by many of today's pundits) that in increasing the national debt "we are stealing from our grandchildren."

(2) Once we remove the above restriction and allow for the possibility that some proportion of the national debt may be held by foreigners, the above conclusions have to be modified. The proportion, if any, held by foreigners may vary from insignificant to significant. It simplifies the essentials if we suppose in what follows that exactly $10 billion of the nation's $200 billion national debt is held by foreigners, leaving it to the reader to generalize for any other portion held by foreigners.

(a) Again, for the very worst case in which the United States government never used a penny of its $200 billion national debt for investments, the additional tax earmarked to pay a five percent interest on the $10 billion held by foreigners, equal to the annual payment of $500 million, is no longer offset by annual interest payments of $500 million of American residents, since the $10 billion of American bonds are now held by foreigners. There is therefore indeed an annual tax "burden" of $500 million.

(b) If, however, we move from this worst case scenario to one in which the government uses no more than $10 billion of its $200 billion of national debt for investing in projects yielding at least five percent per annum, this annual tax "burden" of $500 million is entirely removed—its being offset, or more than offset, by the annual yield of $500 million per annum from the government's investment of $10 billion.

Hence, even though a part of the nation's national debt is held by foreigners, we can be fairly confident that there will be no net tax "burden" even on the existing generation irrespective of the magnitude of the national debt. What is perhaps more to the purpose, in the absence of some devastating catastrophe, we can be absolutely certain that far from the national debt imposing any burden on future generations, they will enjoy material standards greater than we ourselves enjoy today.

8. Finally, a *caveat* against the employment in this connection of the term "burden." It is sad to have to acknowledge that some of my fellow economists, in their writings about the national debt, have unthinkingly and unwarrantably resorted to using the term "burden." I emphasize *unwarrantably* because the word "burden" unavoidably has emotive connotations: nobody is glad to have to bear a burden.

All such emotive terms have no place in positive economics conceived as a social science that restricts itself to disinterested economic analysis. Should an economist believe that increasing the national debt will, *ceteris paribus,* (a) increase taxation, (b) incur a net economic loss (as defined by economists), (c) reduce the income of future generations, and/or (d) does no more than transfer income within the nation from one group to another, then, as a conscientious social scientist, he should declare that his detached analysis has led him to any one or more of these economic consequences of increasing the national debt. Having discharged his duty as an economist, he leaves it to political decision makers to take this information into account in pursuit of their goals.

INFLATION IS CAUSED BY AN EXCESSIVE INCREASE IN THE SUPPLY OF MONEY

1. Just in case there is any uncertainty about it, the supply or quantity of money we are to talk about includes not only the amount of cash held in the economy but also all the bank deposits, whether checking or savings accounts. Moreover, it is generally accepted that—in Western countries at least—the government, or the country's central bank, which alone has the right to create notes and mint coins, has effective control of the money supply, as defined above.

To illustrate one way in which the United States' central bank, the Federal Reserve Bank (the Fed), can change the supply of money is by engaging in "open market operations," that is by buying or selling bonds on the "open market," bonds which are held (for the most part) by large businesses, by banks themselves, and other commercial institutions such as insurance companies, investment companies, and the like. Should the Fed decide to increase the quantity of money in the economy, it will buy, say, Treasury Bonds "on the open market." Suppose it buys $200 million of such bonds. The companies that sold to the bank this $200 million of bonds would receive checks to that amount which they would deposit in their bank accounts at their various commercial banks.

But the story does not end there, because commercial banks also lend money. If, instead, banks merely held money deposited with them so that, at any time, all the money deposited with them could be withdrawn, they would have to charge interest on the deposits they hold in order to stay in business. However, some time long ago, before central banks were thought of, private banks, or those people who acted as banks, soon discovered that, at any one time, only a small proportion of the money they held would be demanded. They could therefore lend a large proportion of the total money they held at a profit—at some competitive rate of interest. Hence they would not charge interest on money deposited with them: indeed, they might even pay interest to induce depositors not to withdraw money without giving several weeks' notice—such interest offered to those holding such deposit accounts being, of course, lower than the interest the banks themselves charged for their loans or overdrafts.

Now if the commercial banks learned that they could safely lend about 80 percent of the money deposited with them, or if the central bank required that all commercial banks not lend more than 80 percent of the total amount of money held, then the initial $200 million paid out by the central bank starts a series of operations that will eventually result in about $1 billion of additional money in the economy. For example, a private bank receiving a check from one or more of its depositors for $20 million from the Fed will lend out 80 percent of it, or $16 million. This $16 million lent to businessmen will be deposited in other banks (possibly some of it deposited in the original private bank). The deposits of these other banks having been increased by $16 million, they too will lend 80 percent of it, or $12.8 million, so creating $12.8 million additional deposits in other banks, as a result of which 80 percent of the $12.8 million is lent out, and so on. Eventually the sum of the amounts lent, along with the initial $200 million created by the Federal Reserve, will have converged to $1 billion. Hence, if all banks lend 80 percent of the deposits they hold, the creation of $x million by the Federal Reserve will create an additional $5x million in the economy.

2. Turning now to the causes of inflation, there can be no doubt that, over past centuries, all recorded inflations were caused by a substantial increase in the quantity of money over a short period. Certainly when the currency used was gold (to a lesser extent, silver), the discovery of large amounts of gold, soon to be circulated as gold coin that vastly increased the expenditure on the current output of goods (which output could not be increased within so short a time-span), could not but raise the level of prices.

However, once central banks, although they might continue to buy gold, were also enabled to create paper money—to create bank notes of various denominations—any deliberate creation by a central bank of paper money would also be able to raise the level of prices and so perhaps to cause an inflation. Indeed, the hyper-inflation that took place in Germany in the early 1920s was maintained by its central bank's creation of ever larger amounts of paper money—of one million Mark bank notes, 100 million Mark bank notes, and so on—until, as was said, the paper itself was worth more than the value of the Marks printed on it. Eventually no one in Germany would accept the Mark as currency, and a monetary reform was necessary, one in which a contrived "guaranteed" Mark was launched.

Be that as it may, since it was generally believed before World War II that market forces alone would operate to maintain or to restore, if not "full employment" at least high employment,[1] any significant increase by a central bank over a short period, it was assumed, would necessarily raise the level of prices and, indeed, might generate inflation.

3. What was often referred to, however, in the early postwar years as monetary policy also included control of interest rates by the central bank. The arch-monetarist himself, the late Milton Friedman, however, would have none of this. For him, monetary policy was to be regarded as the policy of controlling the supply of money alone, not the policy of controlling interest rates. If, therefore, annual economic growth was expected to be 3 percent then a 3 percent increase in the money supply would suffice to maintain unchanged the existing price level. If, however, the annual quantity of money were increased by more than 3 percent, then prices would start rising, and vice versa.

The term monetarist is generally applied not only to the economist who believes that the level of prices, or the rate of inflation, can be controlled by monetary means alone, but to the economist who also believes that a rise in the price level, or in the rate of inflation, is caused *only* by increases in the supply of money—or else that either may be initiated by an increase in the activation of the existing supply of money. This latter possibility would occur if, at a time of high employment, the aggregate expenditure in the economy were to increase simply because consumers and/or businesses were to increase their expenditures so that, in total, such expenditures exceeded the output capacity of the economy. For consumers can always increase their expenditure on finished goods by reducing their savings, or by borrowing on credit, while businessmen can do so either by using their holdings of bank balances, or else by borrowing, so as to increase their investment expenditures or increase the level of their inventories.

In sum, monetarists believe that rising prices are a consequence only of what is called "demand-pull"—a rising demand for goods resulting from increases in the supply of money or from an increased activation of the existing supply of money. In contrast to this belief is the belief that rising prices are, at least primarily, a consequence of "wage-push"—the result, that is, of an increase in the aggregate wage bill by employers in response to workers' claims without there being any corresponding increase in productivity.

Needless to remark, economists might find it agreeable to believe that in any actual inflation, *both* demand-pull and wage-push were involved. Yet the disagreement between the two camps about which of these contrasting factors is the initiating or operative cause of inflation still remains.

4. It transpires that what, in fact, sheds the clearest light on this question about the operative cause of inflation is the revision of the earlier version of monetarism, by what we might call a "Mark 2" monetarism, which was

---

[1]A belief that was challenged, however, in the mid-1930s by the so-called Keynesian Revolution which was premised on the contrary belief: that market forces alone were unable effectively to overcome the distressing levels of unemployment that existed in the developed countries of the West.

advanced in or about the early 1970s—perhaps actuated by the experience of unabating inflation (though at varying rates) in the countries of the West for over 60 years.

Before drawing conclusions from comparing the implications of the Mark 1 and Mark 2 monetarist theories, we may digress briefly to show how the concept of wage-push is used to explain the existence of what is sometimes called "institutional inflation" that is a feature of the modern economy in which the production of services, as distinct from products, form an increasing part. For it is generally recognized that productivity in the service sector, when it occurs at all, does not rise over time as rapidly as it does in the manufacturing and mining sectors of the economy. Efficiency in the performance of secretaries, of masseurs, barmaids, shop assistants, bank tellers, bus and train drivers, cinema and theater staff, teachers, restaurant and hotel personnel cannot be said to rise significantly over time. Yet when it is also observed that, owing to the steady increase in the productivity of workers in industry, such workers' incomes are continually being increased, service personnel regard it as only right and proper that they also should receive corresponding pay rises—the aim being to restore the notional "pay structure" of the economy.

For the economy as a whole, therefore, the overall increase of incomes exceeds the overall increase in real output. Unavoidably then, the prices of manufactured goods must rise, which leads, therefore, to manufacturing workers claiming an increase in their wages simply to cover the now-higher cost of living, and so on. What acts to keep this "institutional inflation" within bounds is the fact that some proportion of the population live on fixed money incomes, and also that workers in the service sectors do not usually succeed in raising their pay in the same proportion as industrial workers.

In addition, the influx of immigrant labor from low-paid countries now also serves as a check to the wage claims of indigenous labor, especially those of less skilled labor.

5. Let us now move to what looks like a quantum leap by monetarists from what we may call the Mark 1 model, in which the existing supply of money determines the *level* of prices, the policy objective being a constant level of prices, to what we may call the Mark 2 model in which now, it is to be the *rate of increase* in the supply of money that is to determine the *rate of inflation*—the consequent objective of policy being a constant rate of inflation. What is more, a critical feature of this Mark 2 model is the part to be played by the level of unemployment.

To come to grips with this last point, let us start with a year in which the annual wage claims of workers exceed the current rate of inflation. Were these wage claims to be conceded by employers, an increase in the existing money supply would be necessary. But suppose the central bank adamantly refused to increase the supply of money that is needed by employers to cover the increase in their payments to workers. Employers would then not be able to meet the higher wage bill required to meet their concession—at least not without reducing some of the workers they employ. Perforce they will indeed have to reduce, to some extent, the number of workers they employ.

But just how many workers must be laid off if the objective is to establish a *constant rate* of inflation? The answer to this question brings us to the connection between the strength of the wage-push of workers and the resulting rate of increase in the money supply. For, in the last resort, it is the increase in the annual supply of money that controls the annual increase in wage *rates*. As for the annual increase in wage *claims,* this depends upon the degree of unemployment in the economy as a whole—the greater the percent of unemployment, the lower the wage claims, i.e. the lower the demand for a rise in wages.

For instance, suppose that a 10 percent rate of unemployment in the economy is needed to maintain workers' claims of an annual increase in wage claims of 4 percent, which claims can only be met by an annual increase of 4 percent in the supply of money. Provided this process continues, the resulting annual 4 percent rate of wage-inflation may be called an *equilibrium* rate of inflation, being one that will continue so long as this 10 percent unemployment is maintained. Possibly in order to promote acceptance of the Mark 2 model, this 10 percent unemployment that is currently necessary to maintain constancy of the rate of wage-inflation is referred to by Friedman and other monetarists as "the natural rate of unemployment."

But this current 4 percent wage-inflation resulting from the 10 percent unemployment is not the only equilibrium possible. Consequently the "natural rate of unemployment" may alter from time to time. For example, if for any reason the central bank were to reduce the annual increase in the supply of money from 4 percent to 3 percent, this reduced annual increase of money would not suffice to meet a wage bill that was increasing annually at 4 percent. Employers would therefore have to lay off a number of workers.

If no more than an annual increase of 3 percent in the supply of money was forthcoming, workers would eventually have to settle for an annual increase in their wage of claims of no more than 3 percent. The militancy of labor, however, may be such that they would not settle for this unless and until unemployment fell to 20 percent. This 20 percent unemployment would therefore now become "the natural rate of unemployment."

At any moment of time, we may conclude, the greater the percent of unemployment the lower the equilibrium rate of wage-inflation. Yet this inverse relationship itself between the percent of unemployment and the rate of wage-inflation (the higher the percent of unemployment, the lower the annual wage claims), referred to as "the Phillips' Curve," is now known to be unstable: it can vary over time and, more obviously, as between countries. It is, therefore, difficult for the monetary authority to maintain a steady rate of inflation. Certainly no specific magnitude may be ascribed to the "natural rate of unemployment," which will vary according to the militancy, or "wage-pushfulness" of labor. The best we can hope for is that the monetary authority will soon be able to alight on that rate of increase of the money supply which produces a tolerable equilibrium rate of inflation corresponding to a *politically* tolerable "natural rate of unemployment."

6. What therefore may be concluded from the above exposition of the Mark 1 and Mark 2 monetarist models, bearing in mind that there is agreement among all economists that any inflation, high or low, can always be terminated simply by curbing the supply of money?

First, if the monetary authority could indeed choose to control prices, and could do so without incurring any untoward consequences, it would surely choose to maintain a constant level of prices—which would entail an increase in the annual supply of money no greater than the annual overall increase in productivity: if real output of the economy increased by 3 percent, a 3 percent increase in the supply of money would suffice to maintain prices constant.

Better still, however, why not hold the quantity of money constant irrespective of increases in productivity. For then the level of prices would decline in proportion to the annual overall increase of output in the economy. Everyone in the country would then benefit equally from the decline in prices including those living on fixed incomes. This is surely more equitable than having wages rise according to the rise in productivity as a result of which workers who benefit are, for the most part, those whose productivity has increased. After all, the increase in the productivity of workers in any particular industry is seldom the result of additional exertion by those workers but the result rather of technological innovations that emerge over time; it therefore being a matter of luck to the workers in whose industry the innovation was applied.

Either a constant level of prices or a declining level of prices would be quite feasible if the economy worked in the way assumed by the earlier Mark 1 model, one in which, it was assumed, the overall level of wages declined without much perturbation until something like full employment were restored.

Second, and once we move on and recognize the stubbornness of the "pushfulness" of workers, at least in the postwar years, events can only be explained by employing the Mark 2 model. In that model we have to accept as a datum the militancy of labor and, therefore, the inverse relationship (as indicated by "the Phillips' Curve") between the percent of unemployment in the economy and the annual wage-inflation. As indicated, however, this relationship is not fixed, but can vary over time according to the increasing or declining militancy of labor.

Certainly the belief that inflation is *caused* by an excessive supply of the quantity of money cannot be vindicated by reference to events in the postwar years. For if indeed that were the cause of inflation, it would follow that any existing inflation can be brought to a halt without any untoward consequences simply by preventing any further increase in the supply of money.

It transpires, however, that we have continued to endure (moderate) rates of inflation every year from 1940 to the present, even though we should all prefer to have stable prices. Thus we cannot escape the economic implications of the Mark 2 model of monetarism that, in the last resort it is prevailing wage "push-fulness" of labor that is responsible for the continuing, though so far moderate, rate of inflation.

7. A cautionary postscript may not be amiss in drawing a conclusion about so slippery a subject as the causes of inflation. I will therefore exert myself to clarify the issues as much as possible.

An existing equilibrium rate of inflation, it has to be conceded, cannot long be maintained without the monetary authority's providing the required rate of increase in the supply of money. But from this obvious fact alone we may not infer that the increase in the supply of money is the direct and operational cause of the resulting inflation—not unless the monetary authority is also completely free to choose the actual increase, or rate of increase, of the supply of money—which is certainly not the case, at least not in the postwar period.

For the fact is that, since World War II, the monetary authority has been constrained to increase the supply of money, or rather to supply the *rate of increase* of money, necessary to support the required rate of wage-inflation that maintains the prevailing "natural rate of unemployment."

To be sure, however, there is not, at any one time, a unique "natural rate of unemployment" but rather a range of possible natural rates, although a range that is effectively limited by what, in a liberal democracy, is politically tolerable. For each of such politically tolerable "natural rates of unemployment" will—as indicated by reference to the prevailing "Phillips' Curve" relationship—correspond to a particular rate of wage-inflation.

Thus a more accurately drawn conclusion would be that, given this limited range of possible "natural rates of unemployment," the monetary authority may indeed act to determine a particular "natural rate," presumably one that also has the sanction of the political authority. Yet once the particular "rate of natural unemployment" is effectively chosen, the monetary authority will unavoidably have to maintain also a particular rate of increase in the supply of money, and therefore to maintain a particular rate of wage-inflation—one that corresponds with that chosen "natural rate of unemployment."

Bear in mind, however, that this correspondence between the rate of wage-inflation and the "natural rate of unemployment" has nothing to do with the monetary authority itself: it is wholly determined by the prevailing militancy (or "wage-pushfulness") of labor.

In sum then, although the monetary authority will have some limited scope in effectively selecting a politically tolerable "rate of natural unemployment," there is no way the monetary authority can opt out of the need to maintain some rate of increase of the supply of money and, therefore, to maintain some rate of wage-inflation.

We may properly conclude, then, that the *operational* factor responsible for the unabating postwar inflation is the wage-push militancy of labor.

THE RATE OF ECONOMIC GROWTH OVER TIME IS A GOOD INDEX OF THE GROWTH OF PEOPLE'S SATISFACTION

1. It is only in recent years that people in the countries of the West have begun to question the desirability of the goal of sustained economic growth which, since the 1950s, has been without exception the top priority of government policy in every country in the world. Yet such has been the impress on men's minds of the conception of economic growth as a limitless source of material plenty that even today an announcement in the media that economic growth in Britain during the last year was, say, three percent, and far exceeding that of France or Germany, can be depended on to raise the spirit of citizens almost as much as the winning by British athletes of Olympic gold medals.

To be sure, for economically poorer countries of the Third World, economic growth is a warrantable goal of policy. If, therefore, we are to understand why it may be less desirable for the richer countries of the West, it is necessary to understand how it is measured, what is included and what is omitted and, more generally, what "bads" are unavoidably produced along with the "goods."

2. The primary measure of economic growth is in terms of the annual increase in value of its GNP (gross national product) or GDP (gross domestic product) in which, at least among the industrialized countries, scores of economists are fully engaged in measuring and forecasting. Since this primary measure is in nominal terms only—in terms, that is, of the prices existing during the year in question (which level of prices is usually higher than that of the preceding years)—the first adjustment that economists make is to express the GNP in "real" terms. This involves the use of an index of annual price changes so as to "deflate" the nominal value of GNP in that year in order that it may be directly compared with the GNP figure of some base year. If, for example, the nominal

GNP for the year 2005 were estimated at $10 trillion, but the price level had doubled since the year 2000, then in order to compare it with the GNP of the year 2000, the estimated $10 trillion in the year 2005 would have to be halved to $5 trillion. If in the year 2000 the estimated GNP had been no more than $4 trillion then, over the next five-year period, there has been only a 25 percent increase in "real" GNP—from $4 trillion to $5 trillion.

3. This section may be omitted, at least on a first reading, by the inquisitive layman since all that follows can be as well understood without having first to learn that the calculation of GNP involves double-counting and is therefore necessarily in excess of *net* national income, NNI—this latter being the annual aggregate of all incomes in the economy, whether calculated as wages, salaries, or profits.

Clearly the growth over time of "real" NNI is more to the purpose. And since all income earned during the year is deemed to be spent either on consumption goods or on investment goods,[1] the resulting annual expenditure on all goods, say it is $2 trillion, is by definition equal to *net* national product, NNP. Hence, NNP can just as well be used as a measure of NNI, its $2 trillion being the sum of its two components, *consumption* expenditure, say $1.88 trillion, plus *net investment* expenditure, say $120 billion.

As it happens, however, an estimation of net investment is more difficult than that of gross investment which consists of net investment (the addition to the stock of capital) and also of the expenditure of firms during the year on what we may call replacement-investment expenditure; that is, of, say, $160 billion on repairs and renewals necessary to maintain the efficiency of the existing stock of capital in the economy—which $160 billion, incidentally, has already been included in the valuation of the $1.88 trillion of consumption goods produced during the year.

Gross national product, being defined as the sum of both consumption expenditure and *gross* investment expenditure during the year, necessarily exceeds NNP by the expenditure on replacement-investment. Using the figures above, the resulting GNP of $2.16 trillion—being the sum of $1.88 trillion of consumption expenditure plus the $280 billion of gross investment expenditure— exceeds the NNP of $2 trillion, by this $160 billion of replacement-investment.

Hence the statement that the calculation of GNP involves double-counting: the $160 billion of replacement-investment being included not only in the consumption expenditure of $1.88 trillion but also again in the gross expenditure on investment, and, hence, also in the GNP of $2.16 trillion.

---

[1]For if people do not spend the whole of their incomes on consumption goods but save, say, $120 billion, this $120 billion saved is, by definition, equal to the expenditure, and therefore also to the output, on investment goods. Thus if the direct expenditure on new plant and machinery happens only to be equal to $80 billion, the remaining $40 billion saved would necessarily result in a $40 billion accumulation of inventories of goods and materials, such accumulation being also regarded as investment expenditure inasmuch as it is an *addition* to the stock of capital in the economy.

4. The estimate of GNP—that is, of annual consumption expenditure and annual gross investment expenditure—can only be a rough estimate of the true GNP. Yet even though the error is appreciable *as a proportion* of the GNP in any year, it does not matter much, provided this error, *as a proportion* of GNP does not vary much from year to year, for we are interested primarily in the change, or growth, over time of the GNP.

It may be mentioned, incidentally, that the magnitude of the error in estimating GNP for any year may be attributed not only to the difficulties in computing the relevant sums but also to institutional factors. For instance, since expenditure on the goods and services produced in the "black economy" are not included in the estimate of GNP, it is to that extent an underestimate. In contrast, since the cost of the goods and services produced in the public sector, which is controlled by the government, are commonly believed to exceed their true worth (say, the value they would fetch if, instead of raising taxes to pay for them, they were to be sold on the market) the GNP measure is an overestimate of the true GNP.

5. A final correction: As an index of the course of material well-being, the change over time of GNP is misleading where no allowance is made for changes in population. Clearly, if the GNP in year *two* turned out to be 20 percent higher than the GNP in the preceding year *one,* there would be no increase in material welfare in the second year if population in that year had also increased by 20 percent.

Thus, the growth of material well-being over time is best measured as the growth over time of *average* real income in the economy, that is, of per capita real income which, in each year is equal to net national product (NNP) divided by the population in that year. As indicated, however, what is actually estimated each year is GNP, this being a proxy for the NNP that is more difficult to measure. But again, this does not signify much since what concerns economists most is the annual change, or annual growth, in per capita real income.

As a postscript it may be mentioned that economists are also interested in the rate of technological progress, either over time or as between two or more countries. The measure used in such cases is output per man-hour (OPMH). The required figure may be obtained directly from the output produced of any one good, or else as a rough overall figure for the economy, by dividing the estimate of GNP in any year by that of the total number of hours worked by the population. It is entirely possible then to discover that although the economy appears to be not working well (say there is a notable decline in GNP compared with the preceding year), technological progress, as measured by OPMH, has indeed taken place.

6. Returning to the growth over the years, of real per capita income, generally regarded as an index of well-being, we are now to discover just how shaky, indeed, just how misleading, it can be, at least once we turn our attention from short-period comparisons—over say 5 or 10 years—to comparisons over long periods of between 50 to 100 years or so. For, although allowance should be

made for the more relevant trends, and for the more relevant changes in conditions in Western economies over long periods, they are in fact seldom made and, indeed, can often be difficult to translate into money terms notwithstanding their importance.

Any index of well-being over time of individual workers should certainly take account of trends in working hours and in conditions of work. Where hours of work are *reduced* over time, the consequent effect in reducing per capita real income ignores the value of the increased leisure enjoyed by workers. Further adjustment is needed insofar as the nature and the conditions of the work itself are altered with the passage of time in many occupations, and can therefore be more or less congenial to workers. On balance, such considerations, could they be measured, would be likely to add to the figure of per capita real income.

Again there are qualitative changes in consumer goods that enhance or reduce their satisfaction over time. For some sorts of manufactured goods, for example radio sets or light bulbs, they have improved over the past few decades. Their decline in prices of course does enter the price index and therefore does enter also into the calculation of real GNP and so into per capita real income. But their improved quality, which adds to their value, does not. On the other hand, there can be a decline in satisfaction over time arising from a loss in the flavor of fruits and vegetables that has resulted from new methods of growth (using pesticides and other chemicals), from transport over greater distances, and from longer periods of storage.

Moreover, the introduction into the economy of novel consumer goods, some of which also have undesirable side effects, along with the withdrawal of other goods that can be a source of regret to some consumers, serves to add further to the penumbra of doubt about the validity of the per capita real income figure.

7. Two other developments over the long period which serve to make the apparent growth in well-being over say the last 50 or 100 years less credible are those of the enlargement of the public sector and of the enlargement in the proportion of women in the workforce.

As pointed out earlier, the goods and services of the public sector are overvalued as compared with those produced by the private sector of the economy. For one thing, government agencies can be overstaffed, and the efficiency of their personnel low, when compared with private industry and commerce. Yet more important, although the willingness of a customer to pay $200 for an item in a retail store is *prima facie* evidence that the item is worth (at least) $200 to him, no such evidence may be adduced to justify government expenditure. For should a man be required to pay an additional $200 in taxes, the additional goods and services he receives from the government, if any, can by no means be assumed to be worth (at least) $200 to him. For in such a case, he is not free to choose such additional public goods: he may not want them at all, or he would rather have other goods that could be bought with his $200. And even though he may appreciate the value of the public goods and services provided by the government, he may himself not want all of them, or he may want them in quite different amounts than those made available by the government.

Yet all the government's output is valued purely by its cost, which cost has to be covered by the taxes levied on citizens. The greater the cost, the greater the measure of its putative contribution to GNP, and ultimately to per capita real income. It follows that the continued expansion over time of the public sector results in a growing over-estimate of GNP and therefore, also, in per capita real income.

Turning to the growth of women's participation in the workforce over the past half century or so, a significant proportion of their contribution to the rising GNP over time is certainly fictitious. For although their services in industry, commerce, and government necessarily add to the value of GNP, the concomitant withdrawal of services once provided in the home is ignored. Some may think that the value lost by the reduction of such services in the home whenever the mother in the home becomes a working mother is indeed important since her presence in the home also confers a sense of security to her children and a likelihood that they will be better behaved and become better citizens. Whether true or not, their value in the home is generally ignored in the calculation of GNP or, occasionally, some crude adjustment for this loss is proposed, such as multiplying an estimate of the total reduction in the number of hours spent in the home by an average hourly market rate of pay for domestic services.

8. It is also of some interest at this stage to consider the implications of a widely accepted definition of net national income, NNI, proposed by the late Sir John Hicks; that it be defined as the expenditure on all goods over the year without reducing the stock of capital. Any reduction in the nation's stock of capital during the year has, therefore, to be counted as a subtraction from the NNI—since if there is a reduction in the stock of capital, some of the goods consumed during that year cannot have been produced in that year but, instead, taken from the stock of capital.

There is little doubt that Sir John had in mind the value only of man-made capital such as plant, machinery, inventories of primary materials, intermediate, and finished goods. But once the stock of capital is extended to include the stock of the earth's natural capital which includes fossil fuels, mineral reserves, ocean fisheries, and tropical forests, not to mention animal and plant species, the NNI so defined for the world, or for individual counties, can be substantially different from a calculation of NNI as conventionally defined. If, as is entirely plausible, we are depleting our natural capital faster than we are accumulating our man-made capital, then the world's NNI, far from growing, may in fact be declining. Certainly the greater the variety of natural assets that are included in the stock of capital available to man—and they should include fresh water reserves, areas of wilderness, of wetlands, and areas of natural beauty, along with the layer of soil that perhaps is gradually being wasted or even poisoned—the less confidence we should have in estimates of economic growth on the conventional definition of the world's NNI or that of any individual country.

9. We turn now to those unavoidable aspects in the production of "goods" that act to reduce the magnitude of estimated GNP, sometimes quite drastically, those we may call "regrettables" and those we may call "inimicals."

Let us start with the "inimicals," or those *negative* external effects,[2] which may be defined as the incidental damage inflicted on the activity or welfare of others that arise from any economic activity or from the goods produced or enjoyed by others. Popular examples include effluent poured into a river by a dye-works, the pollution by motorized traffic of the air in urban areas, the noise created by a neighbor's motorized lawn mower or chain saw, or by low-flying aircraft.

Just as goods are to be measured by the price people are willing to pay for them so "inimicals," or what we may more briefly call "bads," can be measured by the sum people have to be paid to bear with them. Their value ought therefore to be subtracted from the GNP measure—or else added to the *cost* of producing the polluting goods, so increasing their prices (which has the same effect since the resulting higher prices entail a reduction in the "real" value of GNP).

The more potent "bads," however, are impossible or far from easy to measure. These include the damage to human enjoyment and health when fresh air is turned into malodorous or polluted air in urban areas, or the damage to habitation and the health of people arising from floods caused by the destruction of forests, or from the gradual silting by dams and canals, to say nothing of the contamination of the oceans or the depletion of the earth's ozone mantel. The fact that such "bads" may elude measurement does not, of course, prevent our realizing that estimates of the growth over time of per capita real income may be considerably overstated.

10. Possibly even more important in overstating the measured growth in per capita real income is the presence of "regrettables," which can be defined as the additional expenditures on goods or services necessary to maintain the current level of health, protection, or general well-being—or, if that is not possible, to maintain a "tolerable" level thereof.

Thus the expenditure on internal defense, chiefly expenditure on the police force of a country, has grown over time. If, as a result, crime in the country

---

[2]There also exist positive external effects such as the beauty of the front gardens of neighbors, or the pollination of an apple orchard by bees living in the hives of a neighboring garden. Alas, the examples of positive external effects are few whereas the negative ones are many, and sometimes really damaging. For that reason they warrant more of our attention in qualifying the impression given by the growth over time of estimates of real per capita income.

remained unchanged, such expenditure would add nothing to our sense of security. Therefore, the additional expenditure on the police force from 1900 to, say, the year 2000 is regrettable since, in fact, it adds nothing to our feeling of security. Such additional expenditure therefore should properly be subtracted from the estimate of GNP. However, inasmuch as, in some countries, the statistics show something like a fifty-fold increase in crime over the century, which unavoidably increases the level of anxiety in the community, the subtraction from the estimated increase in GNP over the century has to be substantially greater than the increased expenditure on police.

No less important is the military expenditure that over the century has grown enormously in Western countries such as Britain and the United States. It may legitimately be contended that the democracies in each of these countries have in effect collectively chosen to spend an increased amount, generally also an increasing proportion, of their economic resources on defense rather than on any other goods. Yet such an argument is not to the purpose. If, for example, compared with the preceding year, an additional $200 billion is spent by the United States on defense simply in order to maintain parity with the increase in the defense budgets of other nations, it certainly does not follow that American citizens remain as well off as they were in the preceding year—assuming the GNP was the same in each year. For although thanks to this additional (regrettable) expenditure of $200 billion in this current year they will be no worse off in terms of effective defense, they will be undeniably worse off by an unavoidable reduction in their consumption of $200 billion of current goods (arising from a reduction in their disposable income when it is taxed in order to pay for the additional military expenditure).[3]

11. The preceding examples of "regrettables" are by no means the only important ones. The logic employed in rejecting all those additional expenditures on internal and external defense as additions to GNP can be extended to cover other expenditures.

A large proportion of the growth of government expenditure over time is on new agencies that are needed simply to control and monitor developments in a more complex modern economy: to prevent social breakdown or social discord, and to promote the smooth running of the economy. In this category we have to include growing expenditures on the control of motorized traffic, on setting standards for a growing assortment of new consumer goods, on analyzing the toxicity of new chemicals in paints, in cleaning and washing up liquids or powders, and also, therefore, in regulating the amounts and sorts of new chemicals increasingly used by the food industries to impart color, flavor, or preservatives to foodstuffs—also the expenditures needed to disseminate their findings.

---

[3]Should a part of the $200 billion, or even the whole of it, be raised instead by an issue of government bonds, the effect in reducing the expenditure on consumer goods is the same. Alternatively, the government can reduce by $200 billion its provision of certain public goods and services.

But why stop there! Placed in a broad historic perspective, many of the common services provided in the modern economy, for instance those provided by labor unions, by banks, by employment agencies, by welfare workers and counsellors, by travel agencies, by lawyers and accountants, by marriage bureaus or computer-dating facilities, to say nothing of the services provided by the race relations industry or by sex advice clinics, were hardly needed, if at all, in an older, more manageable society of small towns and villages. Such largely regrettable expenditures come into being and grow in importance only as population expands, spreads, and becomes more mobile, as urban areas assume metropolitan dimensions, and modes of living become increasingly complex and more stressful.

Regrettable also are the increased expenditures in the modern economy on travel and commuting that are not enjoyed for their own sake but have become necessary simply as a means of reaching a destination. The same may even be said of a part of the expenditures on vacations insofar as they are undertaken to relieve the increased stress generated by modern living.

12. We can go further. Much of the larger proportion of expenditure on higher education may also be regarded as at least partly regrettable. For the annual investment in much of this higher education is incurred, much like replacement-investment, simply in order to replenish the stock of skilled human capital, without which stock of human capital the modern industrial economy cannot function.

What has been said of the expenditure on higher education can be extended to the information media. A large part of a country's annual expenditure, certainly that on textbooks and professional journals, but to some extent also on newspapers, radio and television sets, and, over the last two decades, on business and home computers, and on mobile phones, have become necessary, not only for vocational training and for coping with a mass of accumulating information, but also for effective participation in the social and political activities of our high-tech civilization. To that extent they are part of the inescapable cost of living in the so-called affluent society.

13. In conclusion, although no one can deny the evidence of the greater material abundance today than, say, 50 or 100 years ago—particularly of our possession of such postwar consumer innovations as electric washing machines, hair dryers, blenders, microwave ovens, refrigerators, televisions, computers, mobile phones, cassettes, i-Pods, and other technological allsorts (that, in the main, are directed to moving us closer to the ideal of instant gratification and instant communication)—such material abundance cannot be interpreted as engendering a growth in individual well-being or in realizing a greater enjoyment of life. Indeed, in a recent television interview, respected academic economists expressed doubts about the belief that (at least within the highly industrialized countries of the West) continued economic growth is making us any happier.

For one thing, we also have to acknowledge that the affluent society today is also liberally sprinkled with those private and public homes and clinics designed to cope with the rising incidence of stress, distress, and family breakdown attributable to a postmodern lifestyle shaped by the relentless demands of technological innovations. Emergency services continue to proliferate. "Hot line" facilities cater to every individual disorder, from drug abuse to post-abortion depression, from suicidal or homicidal impulses to lesbian loneliness.

It is difficult to call a halt to the train of instances of expenditures that appear at first blush to be contributions to real economic growth but which, on further reflection, turn out to be "regrettables"—that is, more like contributions to a higher cost of living. Broadly speaking then, much of the nation's ingenuity is today engaged also in producing sophisticated products and specialized services for meeting those basic needs that were more easily, and sometimes more fully, met by the prewar societies in the countries of the West.

14. Two final observations can only add to the cynical light being cast on the rationale of the goal of economic growth in affluent societies.

First, continued economic growth in the postwar years is culminating unavoidably in making time itself the scarcest resource in Western economies. Apart from the time spent by many in the search for higher remuneration and status, our current purchases from a growing array of modern conveniences and new consumer products and services, the use of which necessarily requires time, continue to make inroads into the limited availability of time. The number of hours each week habitually devoted to "surfing the Net," to watching television programs, or videos or DVDs, also the time often spent choosing from an increasingly daunting variety of goods to buy, shows to see, places to cruise or fly to, cannot but erode the margin remaining for unpre-empted leisure. Few of us escape the feeling that our days are incomplete; that there is never enough time to get through a backlog of activities.

Second, economists have discovered that what matters more to the citizen of the affluent society is not his income *per se,* but his income *relative* to those of others. This so-called "Jones' Effect" (adopted from the common phrase "keeping up with the Joneses") has been confirmed by surveys that reveal, for example, that when an individual is faced with a hypothetical choice of either a 5 percent rise in his own income alone, all other incomes unchanged, or else of a 10 percent rise in his income along with a 10 percent increase in the real incomes of everybody else in the community, the individual almost invariably chooses the former option—even though he would be obviously materially better off choosing the latter option.

Taking this attitude to the limit, then, regardless of whether one believes the growth of GNP is indeed a good proxy for the growth in per capita real income, it follows that if all incomes in the community rise by the same proportion, nobody will feel any better off. And if, which is more realistic, the incomes of some will rise in greater proportion than others, then even where it transpires that everybody's income has been increased to some extent, there will necessarily be some who will feel worse off. The closer we become to this limiting situation, the less rational becomes the social objective of sustained economic growth.[4]

---

[4]A reader interested in a more detailed, albeit a more speculative, critique of economic growth as it affects the quality of people's lives may find time to glance through the pages of my *Costs of Economic Growth,* 2nd ed. (Oxford, United Kingdom: Oxford University Press, 1992).

INDEX